"BY MY SPIRIT"

By
JONATHAN GOFORTH, D.D.

BETHEL
Publishing

1819 S. Main
Elkhart, IN 46516

Printed in the United States of America

CONTENTS

FOREWORD

Occasionally, from the heart and pen of a man of God, a rare and unique book comes which is destined to become a classic in the Christian world. Such is the book, "By My Spirit"—the story of Jonathan Goforth, one of God's great missionary warriors to China in the late 19th century and early 20th century. How God used this giant of his generation to bring revival to the great provinces of China until literally tens of thousands of Chinese were swept into the kingdom of God is a gripping and fascinating story.

As a teenage boy I read the story of Jonathan Goforth of China—the man, his message, and his ministry so thrilled and challenged my heart that I truly believe it was one of God's key instruments in molding and motivating my life toward the Gospel ministry.

Dr. Billy Graham, sensing the tremendous value of this book, has requested that it, along with the other writings of Jonathan Goforth, including the book "How I Know God Answers Prayer" by Rosalind Goforth, be placed in the Billy Graham Memorial Library at Wheaton College, Wheaton, Illinois.

Dr. Leonard DeWitt, president of the Missionary Church of America, recently said, "This is 'must reading' for every minister of the Gospel." He has requested 400 copies of "By My Spirit" so that he might place a copy in the hand of every pastor in the Missionary Church.

Dr. A.W. Tozer, after hearing Jonathan Goforth speak at a missionary conference, observed that there was such a divine radiance upon his countenance that he later said, "It seemed as though I was looking upon the face of God."

Dr. Goforth's daughter, Mary Goforth Moynan, is currently being deluged with invitations to speak in Bible colleges and seminaries across the United States and Canada. Literally thousands of requests are coming in for the Goforth's books, and other thousands are testifying of how these books have blessed and challenged their lives to deeper devotion and Christian service.

It is my conviction that the spiritual dynamics of this book are so powerful that it would be on the priority list of every Bible school and seminary student and minister of the Gospel of Jesus Christ. Its message should not be lost to this generation of Christians who live in the last quarter of the 20th century.

Just as this humble man of God was used to ignite revival flame in the great provinces of China almoist a century ago, I truly believe the Lord will use this rare and exciting book to bring spiritual awakening across the United States, Canada, and to the other nations of the world.

Chaplain Dwight L. Kinman
Director, Love Thy Neighbor Ministries
Tacoma, Washington

CHAPTER I

INTRODUCTORY

In this book we speak of results which are abnormal. If the Almighty Spirit moves in sovereign power on the hearts and consciences of men the outcome must be above the normal. In his introduction to Miss Dyer's *Revival in India,* Dr. A. T. Schofield says: "One thing to be borne in mind is that since the days of Pentecost there is no record of the sudden and direct work of the Spirit of God upon the souls of men that has not been accompanied by events more or less abnormal. It is, indeed, on consideration, only natural that it should be so. We cannot expect an abnormal inrush of Divine light and power, so profoundly affecting the emotions and changing the lives of men, without remarkable results. As well expect a hurricane, an earthquake, or a flood, to leave nothing abnormal in its course, as to expect a true Revival that is not accompanied by events quite out of our ordinary experience."

Perhaps no movement of the Spirit since Pentecost has been so productive of results as the Moravian Revival of the eighteenth century. We read that about noon, on Sunday, August 10th, 1727, "while Pastor Rothe was holding the meeting at Herrnhut, he felt himself overwhelmed by a wonderful and irresistible power of the Lord and sank down into the dust before God, and with him sank down the whole assembled congregation, in an ecstasy of feeling. In this frame of mind they continued till midnight, engaged in praying and singing, weeping and supplication." [1]

The accounts that we have of "the Love Feast in Fetter Lane," London, New Year's Day, 1739, give us an insight into the beginnings of another great movement which originated in that same period. We are told that there

[1] John Greenfield. "Power from on High," p. 24; trans. "Memorial Days of the Renewed Moravian Church."

were about sixty Moravians present at the meeting, together with seven of the Oxford Methodists, namely, John and Charles Wesley, George Whitefield, Wesley Hall, Benjamin Ingham, Charles Kinchin and Richard Hutchins, all of them ordained clergymen of the Church of England. Of that meeting Wesley writes: "About three in the morning, as we were continuing instant in prayer, the power of God came mightily upon us, insomuch that many cried for exceeding joy, and many fell to the ground. As soon as we were recovered a little from that awe and amazement at the presence of His Majesty, we broke out with one voice—'We praise Thee, O God; we acknowledge Thee to be the Lord!'" [2]

I was a student at Knox College when Mr. Moody conducted a three days' series of meetings in Toronto, during the winter of 1883. One of his noon meetings was about as melting as anything I have ever seen. I hardly think there was a dry eye in the assembly that day. No one who attempted to pray could go very far without breaking down.

But though we speak of the manifestations at Pentecost as being abnormal, yet we maintain that Pentecost was normal Christianity. The results, when the Holy Spirit assumed control in Christ's stead, were according to Divine plan. Each one was strengthened with might by His Spirit in the inner man. Christ then did dwell in their hearts by faith, and they were rooted and grounded in love. They were filled unto all the fulness of God, and God did work in and through them above all that they had asked or thought, even unto the "exceeding abundantly." Anything short of that would have defrauded their Lord of His Calvary merits. The purpose of the Holy Spirit was to glorify the Lord Jesus Christ every day from the crowning to the coming. It is unthinkable that He should grow weary in well-doing. My conviction is that the Divine power, so manifest in the Church at Pentecost, was nothing more nor less than what should be

[2] John Greenfield, "Power from on High," p. 35; trans. Wesley's "Journal."

in evidence in the Church today. Normal Christianity, as planned by our Lord, was not supposed to begin in the Spirit and continue in the flesh. In the building of His temple it never was by might nor by power, but always by His Spirit.

The Lord Himself met and foiled Satan after first being filled with the Spirit. And no child of God has ever been victorious over the adversary, unless empowered from the same source. Our Lord did not permit His chosen followers to witness a word in His name until endued with power from on high. It is true that before that day they were the "born-again" children of the Father and had the witness of the Spirit. But they were not the Lord's efficient co-workers and never could be until Spirit-filled. This Divine empowering is for us as for them. We, too, may do the works which our Lord did, yea and the greater works. The Scriptures convey no other meaning to me than that the Lord Jesus planned that the Holy Spirit should continue among us in as mighty manifestation as at Pentecost. One should be able to chase a thousand and two put ten thousand to flight—as of old. Time has not changed the fact that "Jesus Christ is the same yesterday, today and for ever."

"But will it last?" How constantly unbelief puts this question! Of course, the work will last—if man is faithful. When the blood-bought servants of Christ yield Him absolute dominion, all the resources of the Godhead are in active operation for the glory of the Lamb which was slain. The efficacy of the baptism of the Holy Ghost and of fire dies down in any soul only when that soul wilfully quenches it. Did Pentecost last? Did God will that it shouldn't? Pentecost was of God. So was the Wesleyan Revival. It is not God, then, but man whom we must blame for the pitiful way in which the channels of blessing, originating in these great movements, have become clogged up. Can we imagine any one who is determined to co-work with God to the limit of his being asking "Will it last?" At one place in Manchuria, where the Holy Spirit had descended in unusual power upon the people, the Chinese evangelists went and asked the missionary why he had not told them that the Spirit would work so mightily. The missionary penitently replied that he himself had not known that it was possible. How pathetic to come out from "the schools of the prophets" and not realize that the Holy Spirit could endue with power to deliver a prophet's message!

The ministerial association of a certain city in the homeland once invited me to tell them about the Spirit's quickening work in China. In my address I assured them that I had no reason to consider myself any special favorite of the Almighty. What God had done through me in China I was sure He was able and willing to do through them in Canada. Hence that every minister should have the faith and courage to look to God the Holy Spirit to revive His people. I went on to point out that John Wesley and his colleagues were just ordinary men until their hearts were touched by the Divine fire. At that point a Methodist preacher of some note interrupted me. "What, sir!" he exclaimed. "Do you mean to tell me that we don't preach better now than John Wesley ever did?" "Are you getting John Wesley's results?" I asked.

On another occasion I was asked to address a meeting of the Presbyterian Synod in Toronto. I took as my theme the revival at Changtehfu in 1908. I look back to that revival as perhaps the mightiest of the Spirit that I have ever been through. During those wonderful ten days there were seven different times that I was prevented from giving an address owing to the great brokenness among the people. While I was addressing the Synod, a certain theological professor, sitting at a table near-by, looked anything but happy. My account of the Holy Spirit's convicting power over a Chinese audience seemed to put his nerves all on edge. I understand that there was another professor from the same seminary who was sitting in another part of the building, and that he, too, fidgeted in his seat most uneasily. It seems that he finally turned around and hissed—"Rats!" That came perilously near being a sin against the Holy Ghost. By the most liberal allowance, could such prophets be expected to send out from their school young prophets filled with a Holy Ghost message? Can we wonder that spirituality is at so low an ebb throughout Christendom? Thirty-two per cent of the Protestant churches in the United States report no increase in membership for 1927. The church attendance in Britain is not half of what it was twenty-five years ago. There can be no alternative; it is either Holy Ghost revival or apostasy.

We are convinced that the majority of Christian people are living on a plane far below what our Master planned for them. Only the few really seem to "possess their possessions." Nothing can clothe with victorious might but the baptism with the Holy Ghost and with fire: and no one can possess such a baptism without knowing it. So many Church members seem only to have an acquaintance with water baptism, and this notwithstanding what the great Forerunner said: "I baptize you with water unto repentance, but He that cometh after me is mightier than I. . . . He shall baptize you with the Holy Ghost and with fire." Alas! We fear that many leaders know nothing more for themselves and their flocks than "John's Baptism." In spite of all our ecclesiastical pride and self-confidence, just how much of our building would stand the test of fire?

We cannot emphasize too strongly our conviction that all hindrance in the Church is due to sin. It will be seen from the following chapters how the Holy Spirit brings all manner of sin to light. Indeed, the appalling fact is that every sin which is found outside the Church is also found, although perhaps to a lesser degree, within the Church. For fear that some may judge too harshly, we would point out that many of the Chinese churches, of which mention is made, are not even one generation removed from heathenism. At the same time, let us not delude ourselves by thinking that all is well with our old established churches at home. It is sin in individual Church members, whether at home or on the foreign field, which grieves and quenches the Holy Spirit. I imagine that we would lose much of our self-righteousness if we were to find that pride, jealousy, bad temper, back-biting, greed and all their kindred are just as heinous in God's sight as the so-called grosser sins. All sin in the believer, of whatever kind, mars the redemptive work of Christ. The most piercing cries that I have ever heard have come from Chinese Christians, when the Holy Spirit made plain to them that their sin had crucified the Son of God afresh. "Behold, the Lord's hand is not shortened that it cannot save; neither is His ear heavy, that it cannot hear: But your iniquities have separated between you and your God, and your sins have hid His face from you, that He will not hear" (Isa. lix. 1, 2). The filth and blood-guiltiness of the churches can only be swept away by the Spirit of Judgment and of Burning.

In view of the prominence that is given to confession of sin in this book, perhaps it would be as well to make plain my personal views on the subject. Some years ago, I was about to open a series of meetings at an important center in China, when a visiting lady missionary came to me with what she called "a sure plan to move the people." Her idea was that I should first confess my sins, then she would confess hers and afterwards I was to persuade all the missionaries to confess theirs. The Chinese leaders would naturally follow, and she was certain that by that time every one would have broken down. I replied that the Lord had not led me to see things in that light. "If I have hindering sins," I said, "they hinder in Honan, where I am known; and the same applies to yourself. So the sooner we return to our respective fields and get them out of the way the better. To confess our sins before this audience, where we are not known, would only waste valuable time. Besides, who am I that I should urge these missionaries to confess their sins in public, when, for all I know, they may be living nearer to God than I am? The Spirit of God does not need me to act as His detective. If the missionaries here have hindering sins, then we may rest assured that the Spirit will move them to get rid of them. But that is His business, not ours." Never have I witnessed anything more moving than that last meeting when those missionaries, one after another, broke down before the people and confessed to the things that hindered in their lives.

We have a strong feeling that sins committed before conversion are under the blood of God's Holy Son and never should be confessed. To do so is to bring dishonor upon His Calvary sacrifice. We have heard Church-members confess to sins which they had committed previous to their having joined the Church. But such had never really been born again, and the conviction from the Holy Spirit that inspired and accompanied their confessions was usually of an awe-inspiring nature and never failed to move the audience deeply. Moreover, as far as our observation has led us, we have concluded that there must first be deep conviction among the true followers of Christ before any expectation can be entertained of moving the others. From our own experience we are able to state that in every instance where this necessary first stage has been reached, the unconverted in the audience have broken down completely. There could have been no Pentecost unless the one hundred and twenty believers had first reached this stage. The Chinese Christians speak of this work of the Spirit as judgment, but as the "hsiao shen pan" (small judgment), the way still being open to avail oneself of the cleansing efficacy of the precious blood.

We believe, too, that as regards secret sin, i. e. sin which is known only to the individual soul and God, to confess it at the private altar is, as a rule, sufficient to ensure pardon and cleansing. We say, as a rule, because we have known of many, usually such as have been responsible for the salvation of others, e. g. ministers and Church leaders of one sort or another, for whom secret acknowledgment of sin has not been sufficient. Their agonised public confessions have shown plainly that, for them at least, there was only one way of relief.

As to sin against an individual the Scriptures are quite plain. "Therefore, if thou bring thy gift to the altar, and there rememberest that thy brother hath aught against thee; Leave there thy gift before the altar and go thy way; first be reconciled to thy brother, and then come and offer thy gift" (Matt. v. 23, 24). It is vain for us to pray while conscious that we have injured another. Let us first make amends to the injured one before we dare approach God at either the private or the public altar. I am confident that revival would break out in most churches if this were done. Then again, as regards public sins, experience has shown us that these can only be swept away by public confession. True, this amounts to crucifixion; but by our wilful disobedience we have put the Lord of Glory to an open shame, and it is the price that we must pay.

Some years ago, while addressing a large body of ministers and elders in the homeland, we urged that the Divine call was for a greater emphasis upon sin. A few hours later, at a certain ministerial gathering, the subject was brought up, and I understand that in the argument that ensued a large majority decided that the Church had laid too much emphasis upon sin. Man's thoughts, however, are not God's thoughts. Calvary is His emphasis upon sin. Surely, since the sinless Son of God had to be made sin for us an over-emphasis upon sin is in the nature of things impossible. Wasn't it John Wesley, who, as he was passing into the presence of the King, was heard whispering:

> "I the chief of sinners am,
> But Jesus died for me!"

Some mention will be made in these pages of demon possession. We are well aware that it is not a popular subject. When Dr. Nevius's book on "Demon Possession" was published, upwards of thirty years ago, the editor of a noted journal came out with the statement: "Here is another sample of how readily some men let slip the sheet anchor of their reason." Yet, what we have seen with our own eyes has led us to conclude that the slip was not with Dr. Nevius but with the editor, who too readily let slip the sheet anchor of his faith. We again take the liberty of quoting from Dr. Schofield, the famous Harley Street specialist. "I think," he said, "those who know the East cannot doubt that Satan's power there is beyond dispute . . . Lunacy is a general word that covers any departure from sanity, but I think that at times it covers even more. My experience even in England goes to show, and I think the experience of all skilled men directly connected with mental diseases proves conclusively, that here and there one comes across a case that is evidently 'possessed' by some evil spirit. I . . . am one who believes that such cases occur, and still more that the demons may and can and have been 'cast out' and their victims restored to sanity. . . ." [1]

Different ones have termed this work which God has led me into as mere emotionalism. We make no defence other than to quote a few extracts from letters which were written to friends in the homeland by missionaries in Manchuria during the Revival there in 1908.

"Hitherto I have had a horror of hysterics and emotionalism in religion, and the first outbursts of grief from some men who prayed displeased me exceedingly. I didn't know what was behind it all. Eventually, however, it became quite clear that nothing but the mighty Spirit of God was working in the hearts of men."

"Remember that the Chinaman is the most sensitive of men to public opinion, that here were men, and women too, running counter to every prejudice, in the teeth of cherished tradition 'losing face,' and lowering themselves in the public eye, and you will realise a little of the wonder and amazement that filled the missionary body."

"A power has come into the Church we cannot control if we would. It is a miracle for stolid, self-righteous John Chinaman to go out of his way to confess to sins that no torture of the Yamen could force from him; for a Chinaman to demean himself to crave, weeping, the

[1] Helen S. Dyer, "Revival in India," p. 14.

prayers of his fellow-believers is beyond all human explanation."

"We are quite overwhelmed at the wonder of it . . . . We have read of revivals in Wales, in India, and our next-door neighbor, Korea, but when the blessing comes down so fully and freely as it has done these past few days in our midst, it has a new meaning."

"Perhaps you say it's a sort of religious hysteria. So did some of us when we first heard of the Revival. But here we are, about sixty Scottish and Irish Presbyterians who have seen it—all shades of temperament—and, much as many of us shrank from it at first, every one who has seen and heard what we have, every day last week, is certain there is only one explanation—that it is God's Holy Spirit manifesting Himself in a way we never dreamed of. We have no right to criticise; we dare not. One clause of the Creed that lives before us now in all its inevitable, awful solemnity is, *"I believe in the Holy Ghost.'"* [1]

---

[1] "Revival in Manchuria," p. 4; published by the Presbyterian Church in Ireland.

Chapter II

A SEASON OF INTENSIVE PREPARATION

Upon returning to China in the fall of 1901, after having recuperated from the harrowing effects of the Boxer ordeal, I began to experience a growing dissatisfaction with the results of my work. In the early pioneer years I had buoyed myself with the assurance that a seed-time must always precede a harvest, and had, therefore, been content to persist in the apparently futile struggle. But now thirteen years had passed, and the harvest seemed, if anything, farther away than ever. I felt sure that there was something larger ahead of me, if I only had the vision to see what it was, and the faith to grasp it. Constantly there would come back to me the words of the Master: "Verily, verily, I say unto you, he that believeth on Me, the works that I do shall he do also; and greater works than these shall he do . . ." And always there would sink deep the painful realization of how little right I had to make out that what I was doing from year to year was equivalent to the "greater works."

Restless, discontented, I was led to a more intensive study of the Scriptures. Every passage that had any bearing upon the price of, or the road to, the accession of power became life and breath to me. There were a number of books on Revival in my library. These I read over repeatedly. So much did it become an obsession with me that my wife began to fear that my mind would not stand it. Of great inspiration to me were the reports of the Welsh Revival of 1904 and 1905. Plainly, Revival was not a thing of the past. Slowly the realization began to dawn upon me that I had tapped a mine of infinite possibility.

Late in the fall of 1905 Eddy's little pamphlet, containing selections from "Finney's Autobiography and Revival Lectures," was sent to me by a friend in India. It was the final something which set me on fire. On the front page of this pamphlet there was a statement to the effect that a farmer might just as well pray for a temporal harvest without fulfilling the laws of nature, as for Christians to expect a great ingathering of souls by simply asking for it and without bothering to fulfil the laws governing the spiritual harvest. "If Finney is right," I vowed, "then I'm going to find out what those laws are and obey them, no matter what it costs." Early in 1906, while on my way to take part in the intensive evangelistic work which our mission conducted yearly at the great idolatrous fair at Hsun Hsien, a brother missionary loaned me the full "Autobiography" of Finney. It is impossible for me to estimate all that that book meant to me. We missionaries read a portion of it daily while we carried on our work at the fair.

It was at this fair that I began to see evidence of the first stirrings in the people's hearts of the greater power. One day, while I was preaching on I Tim. ii. 1-7, many seemed deeply touched. An evangelist behind me was heard to exclaim in an awed whisper, "Why, these people are being moved just as they were by Peter's sermon at Pentecost." That same evening, in one of our rented halls, I spoke to an audience that completely filled the building. My text was I Peter ii. 24: "He bore our sins in His own body on the tree." Conviction seemed to be written on every face. Finally, when I called for decisions, the whole audience stood up as one man, crying, "We want to follow this Jesus Who died for us." I expected that one of the evangelists would be ready to take my place; but what was my surprise, when I turned around, to find the whole band, ten in number, standing there motionless, looking on in wonder. Leaving one to take charge of the meeting, the rest of us went into an inner room for prayer. For some minutes there was complete silence. All seemed too awed to say anything. At last one of the evangelists, his voice breaking, said: "Brethren, He for Whom we have prayed so long was here in very deed tonight. But let us be sure that if we are to retain His presence we must walk very carefully."

In the autumn of 1906, having felt depressed for some time by the cold and fruitless condition of my out-stations, I was preparing to set out on a tour to see what could be done to revive them. There was a matter, however, between the Lord and myself, that had to be straightened out before He could use me. I need not go into the details. Suffice to say that there was a difference between a brother missionary and myself. I honestly felt that I was in the right. (Such, of course, is very human. In any difference it is always safe to divide by half.) At any rate, the pressure from the Spirit was quite plain. It was that I should go and make that thing straight. I kept answering back to God that the fault was the other man's, not mine; that it was up to him to come to me, not for me to go to him.

The pressure continued. "But Lord," I expostulated, "he came to my study and in tears confessed his fault. So, isn't the thing settled?" "You hypocrite!" I seemed to hear Him say, "you know that you are not loving each other as brethren, as I commanded you to." Still I held out. The fault was the other man's, I kept insisting; surely, therefore, I couldn't be expected to do anything about it. Then came the final word, "If you don't straighten this thing out before you go on that trip, you must expect to fail. I can't go with you." That humbled me somewhat. I did not feel at all easy about going on that long and difficult tour without His help. Well I knew that by myself I would be like one beating the air.

The night before I was to start out on my trip I had to lead the prayer-meeting for the Chinese Christians. All the way out to the church the pressure continued: "Go and straighten this thing out, so that I may go with you tomorrow." Still I wouldn't yield. I started the meeting. It was all right while they were singing a hymn and during the reading of Scripture. But as soon as I opened my lips in prayer I became confused, for all the time the Spirit kept saying: "You hypocrite! Why don't you straighten this thing out?" I became still more troubled while delivering the short prayer-address. Finally, when about half-way through my talk the burden became utterly intolerable and I yielded. "Lord," I promised in my heart, "as soon as this meeting is over, I'll go and make that matter right." Instantly something in the audience seemed to snap. My Chinese hearers couldn't tell what was going on in my heart; yet in a moment the whole atmosphere was changed. Upon the meeting being thrown open for prayer, one after another rose to their feet to pray, only to break down weeping. For almost twenty years we missionaries had been working among the Honanese, and had longed in vain to see a tear of penitence roll down a Chinese cheek.

It was late that night when the meeting closed. As soon as I could get away I hastened over to the house of my brother missionary, only to find that the lights were out and that the whole family were in bed. Not wishing to disturb them I went back to my home. But the difficulty was settled. Next morning, before daybreak, I was on my way to the first out-station. The results of that tour far exceeded anything that I had dared hope for. At each place the spirit of judgment was made manifest. Wrongs were righted and crooked things were made straight. At one place I was only able to spend a single night, but that night all present broke down. In the following year one out-station more than doubled its numbers; to another fifty-four members were added, and to another eighty-eight.

It was only a few months after I had completed this tour that the religious world was electrified by the marvellous story of the Korean Revival. The Foreign Mission Secretary of our Church, Dr. R. P. MacKay, who was visiting in China at the time, asked me to accompany him to Korea. I need hardly say how greatly I rejoiced at such an opportunity. The Korean movement was of incalculable significance in my life because it showed me at first-hand the boundless possibilities of the revival method. It is one thing to read about Revival in books.

To witness its working with one's own eyes and to feel its atmosphere with one's own heart is a different thing altogether. Korea made me feel, as it did many others, that this was God's plan for setting the world aflame.

I had not been in Korea very long before I was led back to the source from which this great movement sprang. Mr. Swallen, of Pingyang, told me how that the missionaries of his station, both Methodists and Presbyterians, upon hearing of the great Revival in the Kassia Hills of India, had decided to pray every day at the noon hour until a similar blessing was poured out upon them. "After we had prayed for about a month," said Mr. Swallen, "a brother proposed that we stop the prayer-meeting, saying, 'We have been praying now for a month, and nothing unusual has come of it. We are spending a lot of time. I don't think we are justified. Let us go on with our work as usual, and each pray at home as he finds it convenient.' The proposal seemed plausible. The majority of us, however, decided that, instead of discontinuing the prayer-meeting, we would give more time to prayer, not less. With that in view, we changed the hour from noon to four o'clock; we were then free to pray until supper-time, if we wished. We kept to it, until at last, after months of waiting, the answer came."

As I remember, those missionaries at Pingyang were just ordinary, every-day people. I did not notice any outstanding figure among them. They seemed to live and work and act like other missionaries. It was in prayer that they were different. One evening, Dr. MacKay and myself were invited to attend the missionary prayer-meeting. Never have I been so conscious of the Divine Presence as I was that evening. Those missionaries seemed to carry us right up to the very Throne of God. One had the feeling that they were indeed communing with God, face to face. On the way back to our host's residence, Dr. MacKay was silent for some time. I could see that he was greatly agitated. Finally, with deep emotion, he exclaimed: "What amazing prayer! You missionaries in Honan are nowhere near that high level."

What impressed me, too, was the practical nature of the movement. I soon saw that this was no wild gust of "religious enthusiasm," dying with the wind upon whose wings it had been borne. There were, of course, the usual outward manifestations which inevitably accompany such phenomenal outpourings of spiritual power. But beyond all that was the simple fact that here were tens of thousands of Korean men and women whose lives had been completely transformed by the touch of the Divine fire. I saw great churches, seating fifteen hundred people, so crowded that it was found necessary to hold two services, one for the men and one for the women. Every one seemed almost pathetically eager to spread the "glad tidings." Even little boys would run up to people on the street and plead with them to accept Christ as their Savior. One thing that especially struck me was their abounding liberality. The poverty of the Koreans is proverbial. Yet one missionary told me that he was afraid to speak to them about money; they were giving so much already. Everywhere I saw an evident devotion for the Holy Word. Every one seemed to carry a Bible. And permeating it all was that marvellous spirit of prayer.

On our way back to Honan, Dr. MacKay and I took the northern route through Manchuria. There was but one dominant thought in my mind. Since God was no respecter of persons, He was surely just as willing to bless China as Korea. I resolved that this would be the burden of my message wherever I went. At Mukden I told the story of the Korean Revival, one Sunday morning, to a large congregation. They seemed to be deeply moved, and asked me to come back in February of the following year to conduct a week of special meetings. At Liaoyang the story met with the same warm reception, and here again an invitation was extended to me to return next year and give a series of revival addresses. Continuing southwards, we came to Peitaiho, where once again I told the story, this time to a large body of missionaries. A profound impression was made. A number of the missionaries got together and resolved that they would pray for Revival until a movement similar to that in Korea had swept over China.

Upon my arrival at Changtehfu, I found a letter awaiting me from the missionaries of Kikungshan, insisting that I go and tell the story to them, too. On the Sunday evening that I gave the address at Kikungshan I noticed, as I ended, that I had gone considerably over the rather generous time limit which I had set myself. Not wishing, therefore, to detain the people any longer, I omitted the closing hymn and simply pronounced the benediction. But, to my surprise, for at least six minutes no one stirred. The stillness of death seemed to pervade the assembly. Then gradually suppressed sobs became audible here and there. In a little while, missionaries were rising to their feet and in tears confessing their faults one to another. It was late that night when we finally scattered to our homes.

A conference, with a schedule of prepared addresses, had been planned for the ensuing week. But when the missionaries met on the Monday morning it was decided that we should throw the prepared schedule aside and just continue in prayer and along whatever line the Lord should move us. Never have I passed more wonderful days among my missionary brethren in China. Before we finally separated to our different stations, scattered throughout the length and breadth of the country, we resolved that, no matter where we were or what we were doing, we would pray every day at four o'clock in the afternoon until the Divine blessing fell upon the Church of China.

CHAPTER III

THE BEGINNING OF THE MOVEMENT IN MANCHURIA

WHEN I started on the long journey to Manchuria in February, 1908, I went with the conviction in my heart that I had a message from God to deliver to His people. But I had no method. I did not know how to conduct a Revival. I could deliver an address and let the people pray, but that was all.

On the evening of my arrival at Mukden, my missionary host and I were talking together in his study. Naturally I was keyed up to the highest pitch at the prospect of what lay ahead. My host, however, seemed peculiarly indifferent to the thought of Revival. This evening, of all evenings, he chose to impress upon me the enlightened nature of his theological views. "You know, Goforth," he said, "there's an awful windbag in your mission. What's his name? Mac—something?" "Is it MacKenzie?" I asked. "Surely you can't mean him? Why, that man is anything but a windbag. He is considered one of the leading theologians in China." "No," he said, "it's not MacKenzie. Oh, yes, I remember—it's MacKay." "But MacKay is our Foreign Secretary," I replied, "and an address from him would be more than acceptable in any land." "Well," he continued, "I heard him down at the Shanghai Conference. Why, man, his theology is as old as the hills." "I think we had better stop right here," I said, "my theology is just as old as MacKay's. In fact, it is as old as the Almighty Himself."

I learned, too, that the wife of my host was not in sympathy with the meetings, and had left the day before my arrival to visit some friends in a neighbouring city. I couldn't help but think to myself that, if the attitude of this home were reflected in the minds of the other missionaries, then the outlook for Revival was, to say the least, not very encouraging.

But there were further disappointments in store for me. When the invitation had been extended to me, the preceding year, to conduct a series of special meetings in Mukden, I had stipulated as to the conditions of my acceptance, first, that the two branches of the Presbyterian Church in Mukden, namely the Scottish and the Irish, should unite for the services; and, secondly, that the way should be prepared by prayer. Imagine my disappointment, therefore, when I found, upon enquiry, that not one extra prayer-meeting had been held. But the last straw which was laid on the back of my already wavering faith was when I learned, after the evening service on the opening day, that the two Presbyterian bodies had not united. I went up to my room, knelt down by my bed, and, unable to keep the tears back, I cried to God: "What is the use of my coming here? These people are not seeking after Thee. They have no desire for blessing. What can I do?" Then a voice seemed to come right back to me: "Is it your work or Mine? Can I not do a sovereign work? 'Call upon Me and I will answer thee, and will show thee great things, and difficult, which thou knowest not'" (Jer. xxxiii. 3, R. V.).

Early next morning one of the elders came to see me. As soon as we were alone he burst out weeping. "In the Boxer year," he said, "I was treasurer of the Church. The Boxers came and destroyed everything, the books included. I knew I could lie with safety. There were certain Church funds in my keeping which I swore I had never received. Since then I've used the money in my business. Yesterday, during your addresses I was searched as by fire. Last night I couldn't sleep a wink. It has been made plain to me that the only way that I can find relief is to confess my sin before the Church and make full restitution "

After my address that morning the elder stood up before all the people and laid bare his sin. The effect was instantaneous. Another member of the session gave vent to a piercing cry, but then something seemed to hold him back and he subsided without making a confession. Then many, moved to tears, followed one another in prayer and confession. All through the third day the movement increased in intensity. The missionary, at whose home I was staying, said to me: "This amazes us. It is just like the Scottish Revival of 1859. Hadn't you better drop your planned addresses and just let us have thanksgiving services from now on?" "If I understand the situation aright," I replied, "you are far from the time of thanksgiving yet. I believe that there is still much hidden sin to be uncovered. Let me go on with my addresses, and after I am through you can have all the thanksgiving meetings you like."

On the fourth morning an unusually large congregation had assembled. The people seemed tense, expectant. During the singing of the hymn immediately preceding my address an inner voice whispered to me: "The success of these meetings is phenomenal. It will make you widely known, not only in China but throughout the world." The human in me responded, and I experienced a momentary glow of satisfaction. Then immediately I saw that it was the evil one, at work in his most insidious form, suggesting that I should divide the glory with the Lord Jesus Christ. Fighting the temptation down, I replied: "Satan, know once and for all that I am willing to become as the most insignificant atom floating through space, so long as my Master may be glorified as He ought." Just then the hymn ended, and I rose to speak.

All through that address I was acutely conscious of the presence of God. Concluding, I said to the people: "You may pray." Immediately a man left his seat and, with bowed head and tears streaming down his cheeks, came up to the front of the church and stood facing the congregation. It was the elder who, two days before, had given vent to that awful cry. As if impelled by some power quite beyond himself, he cried out: "I have committed adultery. I have tried three times to poison my wife." Whereupon he tore off the golden bracelets on his wrist and the gold ring from his finger and placed them on the collection plate, saying: "What have I, an elder of the Church, to do with these baubles?" Then he took out his elder's card, tore it into pieces and threw the fragments on the floor. "You people have my cards in your homes," he cried. "Kindly tear them up. I have disgraced the holy office. I herewith resign my eldership."

For several minutes after this striking testimony no one stirred. Then, one after another, the entire session rose and tendered their resignations. The general burden of their confession was: "Though we have not sinned as our brother has, yet we, too, have sinned, and are unworthy to hold the sacred office any longer." Then, the deacons one by one got up and resigned from their office. "We, too, are unworthy," they confessed. For days I had noticed how the floor in front of the native pastor was wet with tears. He now rose and in broken tones said, "It is I who am to blame. If I had been what I ought to have been, this congregation would not be where it is to-day. I'm not fit to be your pastor any longer. I, too, must resign."

Then there followed one of the most touching scenes that I have ever witnessed. From different parts of the congregation the cry was heard: "It's all right, pastor. We appoint you to be our pastor." The cry was taken up until it seemed as if every one was endeavouring to tell the broken man standing there on the platform that their faith and confidence in him had been completely restored. There followed a call for the elders to stand up; and as the penitent leaders stood in their places, with their heads bowed, the spontaneous vote of confidencee was repeated, "Elders, we appoint you to be our elders." Then came the deacons' turn. "Deacons, we appoint you to be our deacons." Thus were harmony and trust restored. That evening the elder whose confession had had such a marked effect was remonstrated with by one of his friends. "What made you go and disgrace yourself and your family like that?" he was asked. "Could I help it?" he replied.

It was a great joy to me to note the change that took place during the meetings in the attitude of my missionary host. One morning, while prayers were being offered up for different people, this missionary ran forward, crying:

"Oh, pray for us missionaries; for we need it more than any of you." His wife, whose indifference to the meetings we have already noted, returned from her visit several days before the services ended. But it was not too late. Her heart was won, and she became, if anything, even more consecrated than her husband.

On the last day of the meetings the native pastor said to the people: "You people know how many elders and members of this congregation have drifted away. Oh! if there were only some way of bringing them back." At these words the whole audience stood up as one man and united in prayer for the lost sheep. They prayed as if the souls of those wandering ones were the only things that mattered. It was like a mother pleading for the return of her rebellious son. That year hundreds of members, who had drifted away, returned to the fold. Most of them confessed that they did not think that they had ever really been converted before.

There was an elder in the Liaoyang congregation who, a short time before my arrival, had moved to new lodgings on the Sabbath Day. The missionary had called upon him and remonstrated with him, pointing out how ill it befitted his position to set such a bad example. The elder had become greatly incensed, and had claimed that Sunday had been the only day in which he had time to effect the change. On the morning of the second day this elder broke down before the congregation and confessed his sin. He had had time to move during the week, he said; but he had coveted the use of the Lord's Day. Some time after my departure from Liaoyang, the elder held a series of special meetings with the High School boys. The results, I am told, were truly extraordinary.

After the elder's confession on the second day, the pressure increased rapidly. On the morning of the fifth day, one old backslider cried out in agony: "I murdered him." Then he gave his confession. It appeared that he was a doctor. A neighbour and himself had been at bitter enmity with each other. One day he was called in to prescribe some medicine for his neighbour, who had been taken sick. He had given him poison and the man had died. The effect of that revelation can be more easily imagined than described. In a few minutes the whole congregation seemed to be in the throes of judgment. People everywhere were crying out for mercy and confessing their sins.

On the way back to the mission compound after the final meeting, Mr. Douglas, the resident missionary, said to me: "I am humbled to the dust. This is the Scottish Revival of 1859 re-enacted before my eyes. Although I was not there myself I have often heard my father tell about it. He said that the people would work in the field all day, hurry back home, have something to eat, and then rush off to the church where they would stay till midnight. But my weak faith wouldn't allow me to expect anything like that here." He then handed me a letter which he had received several weeks before from Dr. Moffatt, of Pingyang, Korea. "I thought I would let you know," it read, "that while the meetings at Liaoyang are going on, my people here, three thousand strong, will be praying that God's richest blessing may come to you."

The revival at Liaoyang was the beginning of a movement which spread throughout the whole surrounding country. Bands of revived Christians went here and there preaching the Gospel with telling effect. At one outstation there was a Christian who had a notoriously bad son. During the meetings that were held by one of the revival bands at his village the young man quite broken up, confessed his sins and came out strongly for Christ. His conversion produced a remarkable effect upon the whole village. Heathen would say to each other on the streets: "The Christian's God has come. Why, He has even entered that bad fellow, and driven all the badness out of him. And now he's just like other Christians. So, if you don't want to go the same way you had better keep away from that crowd."

In that same village there was a Christian who had borrowed a considerable sum of money from a heathen neighbour a number of years back; which debt, as he confessed later, he had had no intention of ever repaying. But, as a result of the testimonies of the revival band, he was led to consecrate his life anew, and, as the first step, he calculated the compound interest on his debt, went to his creditor and repaid him in full.

At another village in the same region there was a certain notorious character who was renowned far and wide for his phenomenal success at the gambling table. One day this man saddled his donkey and started up north to collect some money from certain of his victims who lived in that direction. But he got no further than the outskirts of the village when the donkey stopped. The gambler kicked and beat and cursed it, but all to no avail. The animal was adamant. North it would not go. Then it occurred to the man that there were some villages to the south where money was owing him. So he turned the donkey around and it started off without any trouble. Everything ran smoothly enough until they came to a cross-road where one branch went south-east and one south-west. The gambler had in mind a village which lay along the road running south-west. It was upon that road, therefore, that he endeavoured to urge his steed. But again the donkey had decided differently. It made quite clear to its master that if it were to budge another inch the route followed must be the one running south-east. Blows and entreaties were alike of none effect. "All right, have your own way," said the man at last, disgustedly, "and anyway, if I am not mistaken, there are some who owe me money down that way, too." So they proceeded on their journey.

In a little while they came to a village. They continued up the main street until they were directly opposite a little Christian church. Here the donkey stopped, and nothing the man could do could make it move a foot farther. In despair the man alighted. Now it happened that some of the Christians who had attended the Liaoyang meetings were holding a service in the church. The gambler, standing nonplussed outside the door, heard the sound of singing. His curiosity aroused, he decided to enter and see what it was all about. The power of God was present there that day. He heard this one, in tears, confessing his sins, and that one, with radiant face, telling of the joy and peace that had come into his life. Soon a powerful conviction came over the man. He stood up and confessed his sins and told how he had been led to the meeting. "How can I help but know," he cried, "that this is the voice of God?"

CHAPTER IV

FURTHER TRIUMPHS OF THE SPIRIT IN MANCHURIA

SHORTLY after my arrival at Kwangning one of the missionaries said to me: "Reports have come to us of the meetings at Mukden and Liaoyang. I thought I had better tell you, right at the beginning, that you need not expect similar results here. We're hard-headed Presbyterians from the north of Ireland at this place, and our people take after us. Even our leaders won't pray unless you ask them to individually. And as for women praying —that's quite unheard of!" "But I never ask any one to pray," I replied; "I only expect a man to pray as the Lord moves him." "Very well," said the missionary, "be prepared for a Quakers' meeting."

The following morning, after I had given my address, I said to the people: "Please let's not have any of your ordinary kind of praying. If there are any prayers which you've got off by heart and which you've used for years, just lay them aside. We haven't any time for them. But if the Spirit of God so moves you that you feel you simply must give utterance to what is in your heart, then do not hesitate. We have time for that kind of praying. Now, the meeting is open for prayer." Immediately eight men and women got up, one right after the other, and prayed. The missionaries were astounded. They confessed they had never seen anything like it. After the evening address, that same day, over twenty men and women followed one another in prayer. Next day even the schoolboys and schoolgirls were taking part.

On the third day the eagerness to pray was so strong that no one could get started unless he began his prayer before the one preceding him had said "Amen." Once a lady missionary whispered to me: "The men are praying so rapidly that the women can't open their mouths.

Won't you tell them to hold back for a little while and give the women a chance?" I replied that at the close of every address I, as far as possible, committed the control of the meeting to the guidance of the Holy Spirit, and therefore did not feel justified in interfering. Presently, however, a woman did get started, and for fifteen minutes or so the men had to hold their peace. After one such meeting a visiting missionary was heard to remark, "I've never heard such praying as that before. Why, it just seemed as if it had suddenly dawned upon those people that a way of access had been opened to the Throne of Grace, and they were eager to get in all their confessions and petitions before the day was closed."

After the evening meeting, on the third day, a few of us missionaries were conversing together. "I can't understand how it is," said one, "that our Chinese leaders are so silent these days. So far all the praying has been done by the ordinary church members. In the prayer-meetings that were held before Mr. Goforth came the leaders didn't hold back at all. Why, then, should they be so silent now?" "I think you can count upon it," I said, "that there is a hindrance among your leaders. It is sin that makes them dumb." Immediately one of the lady missionaries took me up. "Oh, come now, Mr. Goforth," she said, "you surely don't expect us to believe that there are such sinners among our leaders as there were at Mukden and Liaoyang. Why, we would be ashamed of ourselves, if there were."

On the fourth day we began the afternoon meeting about four o'clock. Following my address the same deep intensity in prayer became evident. After prayer had continued for about half an hour a strange thing happened. More than half the congregation went down on their knees. Strange, I say, because it was a Presbyterian Church, and the people had always been accustomed to stand while praying. Feeling, however, that it was the direction of the Spirit, I intimated that they might all go down on their knees if they wished—and they did.

Then an elder stood up and said to another elder, who was seated on the platform: "In the session meetings it was always my bad temper that was the cause of trouble. Please forgive me." And the elder who was thus addressed cried back: "Please don't say any more. I'm just as much at fault as you are. It's you who should forgive me."

A few minutes of silence followed, and then a man rose from his knees and in a clear voice, though he was bordering on tears, began to pray. For several days I had been taking note of the man, although I did not know who he was. He had a strong, intelligent face, upon which anxiety was plainly written. "O God," he cried, "you know what my position is—a preacher. When I came to these meetings I determined that, come what would, I would keep my sins covered up. I knew that if I confessed my sins it would bring disgrace not only upon myself but upon my family and my church. But I can't keep it hidden any longer. I have committed adultery. . . . But that is not all. In one of the out-stations a deacon committed a horrible sin which hindered Thy cause. My plain duty was to report the affair to the missionary, but the deacon bought me a fur garment, and I accepted it and it sealed my lips. But I can't wear it any longer." With that he tore off the garment and flung it from him as if it had been the plague. Then he continued to pray with glowing intensity until the whole audience was swept as by fire. Even the smallest children began to cry out for mercy. The meeting did not break up until ten o'clock that night, having lasted six full hours.

At this meeting there was an unusually large number of outsiders, their curiosity doubtless having been aroused by the strange rumours that were current throughout the district. As their numbers kept increasing, Mr. H—— became alarmed and herded them together near the door, so that if they got obstreperous he could rush them out. But his fears were groundless, for no sooner had the movement begun among the Christians than they, too, came under conviction, got down on their knees and began crying for mercy.

Another remarkable thing about the movement on that memorable evening was the way in which conviction came over certain Christians who, for some reason or other, were not able to attend the meeting. Among these was a prominent member of the session. About the time when the movement in the church was at its height, this elder began to suffer intense pain, so much so, in fact, that he became convinced that he was going to die. As he lay on his bed, writhing in his agony, his deadened conscience was stirred, and he was reminded of the time when he had been overseeing the building of the street chapel. There were so many pieces of timber and so much brick and other material which he had coveted and which he had used in the construction of his own house. Not being able to write himself, the wretched man had his son make a list of the things which he had stolen, and he made the young man promise that he would read the confession aloud to the congregation on the following day. Next morning, however, the elder was better. Courageously he went himself and gave his confession, creating a deep impression upon the whole Church.

After the meetings, bands of revived Christians toured the surrounding country. At every out-station that was visited, except one, a deep spiritual movement resulted. When the bands returned to the city this particular place was made the occasion for special prayer. Then another band was sent to the village, and a movement set on foot which quite eclipsed anything which had been seen in any of the other out-stations.

In a village, not far from Kwangning, there was a young fellow who enjoyed a peculiarly notorious reputation. His father was a Christian, which fact served but to emphasise the scandal of his own life. Not to mention his other nefarious activities, he was associated with a company of bandits who made of his home a sort of headquarters where plans could be discussed and loot divided. Rumors of this finally reached the ears of the local mandarin, who had the young fellow seized and put under torture in order to extract a confession from him. Many forms of torture were resorted to, but to no avail. He would reveal nothing. At last, in despair, the mandarin invited one of the missionaries to try and see what he could do. The missionary pleaded and argued with the man, but still he refused to open his mouth. His courage, in the face of what he suffered at the hands of the authorities, was remarkable. "Go ahead and kill me," he would say to the mandarin, "but you needn't think you can make me speak. You've got a spite against me because my father is a Christian. That's your only excuse for arresting me."

So impressed was the mandarin by the bold stand taken by the young fellow that he began to doubt whether after all he was really guilty. At any rate, he decided to let him go. Not long afterwards, a revival band from Kwangning visited the district. After much coaxing the young desperado was induced to attend one of the meetings. He came under conviction and stood up before his fellow-villagers and confessed everything. Then he went to Mr. H——, who was in charge of the band, and begged that he might be allowed to accompany him from place to place and tell his story. Mr. H—— confessed to me later that he was a trifle dubious at first about accepting the man, so notorious had been his reputation. But, finally, he agreed to take him on. And certainly he had no reason to regret his decision. The young ex-bandit became the life of the band. Every one who heard his testimony seemed to be moved.

From the very first meeting at Chinchow a movement began to develop. There was the same intense prayer spirit, the same anxiety to get rid of hindering sin which had been so marked at the other stations. On the morning of the third day I received an anonymous letter in which the request was made that we should have special public prayer for a preacher and his wife (their names being mentioned), who, by their violent quarrelling, were hindering the work at one of the mission's most important out-stations. My informant mentioned also a prominent

deacon and his brother who, through the same fault, had
brought the work at another station to a standstill. Emphasis was laid upon the gravity of the matter, it being
pointed out that whereas many of the ordinary church-
members had broken down and confessed, the leaders
were still holding studiously aloof.   My correspondent
concluded with the suggestion that I should mention the
offending ones by name, so that general intercession could
be made for them.

While I was glad, in a way, to have some idea of where
the hindrance lay, yet I realised, of course, that to follow
out the suggestion mooted in the letter would be a serious
blunder. I had committed the movement to the control
of the Holy Spirit; it was not for me to interfere. Immediately after my address that afternoon, a man rose and
offered up a heart-broken prayer of confession. It was
his temper, he declared, which had estranged him from
God. So violent was it, he said, that his wife didn't dare
live in the same room with him. This was the preacher
concerning whom my anonymous correspondent appeared
to have such anxiety. As soon as the meetings were over
the repentant leader went back home and made things
right with his wife. And not long afterwards, I am told,
a Revival broke out at his station.

Scarcely had the preacher ended his confession when
another arose and declared that his temper was so vile
that it was impossible for his own brother to get along
with him. He had tried, he said, to manage his brother
with force and anger rather than with love. At that a
young man came running from another part of the
church and threw himself down at the other's feet, weeping and begging for forgiveness. It was the deacon and
his brother.

I will just mention one other incident. Several months
before my arrival at Chinchow, the lady doctor at the mission hospital had suddenly awakened to the realisation
that a considerable quantity of valuable medicine was dis-
appearing, so to speak, right under her very nose.   She

called in her assistant and, pointing to the room where the medicine was kept, she said: "You and I are the only ones who have charge of the key to that room. A lot of medicine is missing. Have you any explanation to offer?" "What!" cried the girl, becoming greatly incensed, "you accuse me of being a thief!" And she left the mission, giving the impression that her proud spirit could not brook the injustice which had been done to her. The facts of the rather sordid story soon became known. It appeared that the girl had stolen the medicine under pressure exerted by her father, an old, back-slidden Christian and a doctor of some note in the city. The man had attracted considerable patronage to himself by advertising throughout the city that he dealt only in "expensive foreign medicines."

Each day during the meetings a message was sent to the girl, inviting her to come, and saying that her friends were constantly remembering her in prayer. But it was not till the last day that she finally put in an appearance. She was pointed out to me at the forenoon meeting. Immediately I was impressed by her fine appearance and by the strength of character so evident in her face. She could not have been more than twenty. All through the service she sat rigidly in her seat with a defiant look on her face, as much as to say, "I have a will of my own. Say what you will, I have nothing to confess."

At the noon hour the missionaries offered up special prayer that the Lord would bring the girl back to the afternoon meeting. She was sitting in the front row when I arrived to open the service. About halfway through my address her head went down and the tears began to flow. In the open session for prayer that followed my address the men completely monopolised the floor. Feeling that this girl simply must be given a chance to get rid of the burden which so plainly was weighing upon her, I announced a hymn. At its close I said to the men: "Do be patient, brethren, and let the women have an opportunity to pray for a little while." Then this young woman stood up and faced the congregation and said: "I have much to confess. But I'm not worthy to make my confession standing up. I must kneel." So she knelt down on the platform and poured out the whole miserable story. About two months later I learned of her death. Some internal malady had been sapping her life-blood and had finally carried her away. What a tragedy might it have been if that young woman had resisted the Spirit of God and had gone to meet Him with the unpardoned sin.

Dr. Walter Phillips, who was present at two of the meetings in Chinchow, writes: "It was at Chinchow that I first came into contact with the Revival. Meetings had been going on there for a week, hence, I was ushered into the heart of things unprepared, and in candour, I must add, with a strong temperamental prejudice against 'revival hysterics' in every form, so that mine is at least an unbiased witness.

"At once, on entering the church, one was conscious of something unusual. The place was crowded to the door, and tense, reverent attention sat on every face. The very singing was vibrant with new joy and vigour. . . . The people knelt for prayer, silent at first, but soon one here and another there began to pray aloud. The voices grew and gathered volume and blended into a great wave of united supplication that swelled till it was almost a roar, and died down again into an undertone of weeping. Now I understood why the floor was so wet—it was wet with pools of tears! The very air seemed electric—I speak in all seriousness—and strange thrills coursed up and down one's body.

"Then above the sobbing, in strained, choking tones, a man began to make public confession. Words of mine will fail to describe the awe and terror and pity of these confessions. It was not so much the enormity of the sins disclosed, or the depths of iniquity sounded, that shocked one. . . . It was the agony of the penitent, his groans and cries, and voice shaken with sobs; it was the sight of men forced to their feet, and, in spite of their struggles, impelled, as it seemed, to lay bare their hearts that moved one and brought the smarting tears to one's own eyes. Never have I experienced anything more heart-breaking, more nerve-racking than the spectacle of those souls stripped naked before their fellows.

"So for hour after hour it went on, till the strain was almost more than the onlooker could bear. Now it was a big, strong farmer grovelling on the floor, smiting his head on the bare boards as he wailed unceasingly, 'Lord! Lord!' Now a shrinking woman in a voice scarce above a whisper, now a wee laddie from the school, with the tears streaking his piteous grimy little face, as he sobbed out: 'I cannot love my enemies. Last week I stole a farthing from my teacher. I am always fighting and cursing. I beseech the pastor, elders and deacons to pray for me.' And then again would swell that wonderful deep organ tone of united prayer. And ever as the prayer sank again the ear caught a dull undertone of quiet sobbing, of desperate entreaty from men and women, who, lost to their surroundings, were wrestling for peace."[1]

The Christian community in Shinminfu had been terribly persecuted during the Boxer uprising of 1900. Fifty-four had suffered martyrdom. The ones who were left prepared a list, containing 250 names in all(of those who had taken part in the massacre. Some day, it was hoped, the way would be opened for them to wreak on these full and complete revenge.

The crisis was reached here on the afternoon of the fourth day. Again I had the feeling that I was a witness at a scene of judgment. After the meeting had continued for about three hours I pronounced the benediction. Immediately cries went up from all over the audience: "Please have pity on us and let the meeting go on. For days we haven't been able to sleep. And it will be just the same for another night if you don't give us a chance to get rid of our sin now." I asked a lady missionary to take the women and girls over to the girls' school and to continue

[1] "Revival in Manchuria," pp. 20-22.

with them there until the movement subsided. I did not
see any hope of the meeting ever ending otherwise.

As the women and girls were filing out, one of the evangelists came and knelt down in front of the platform. He
confessed several sins with seeming genuineness, but still
the burden which was plainly weighing upon him appeared
to be in no way removed. I said to him: "Since you have
confessed your sins, God is faithful and just to forgive you
your sins and to cleanse you from all unrighteousness. Go
in peace." "But I haven't confessed the worst sin of all,"
he cried brokenly. "I won't forgive." "Then, of course,"
I replied, "God can't forgive you." "But it is humanly impossible for me to forgive," he went on. "In the Boxer
year a man came and murdered my father, and ever since
then I've felt that it was my duty to avenge his death. Just
the other day a friend of mine wrote to me, saying,
'Where's your filial piety? Your father has been murdered, and you are living without avenging him. You aren't
worthy to be my friend!' Why, I simply can't forgive that
man. I must destroy him." "Then I am afraid," I said,
"that it is clear from God's Word that He can't forgive
you." He did not say anything more, but just continued
on his knees, weeping.

Then a schoolboy got up and said: "In 1900 the Boxers
came to my house and killed my father. All along I have
felt that I should grow up and avenge that wrong. But
during these last few days the Holy Spirit has made me so
miserable that I haven't been able to eat or sleep or do
anything. I know He is urging me to forgive the murderers for Jesus' sake. Do pray for me." Another boy
told how the Boxers had come to his home and killed his
father and mother and elder brother. In fact, as many as
nine boys got up in that way and told how their mothers
and fathers and brothers and sisters had been murdered
before their very eyes, and how that ever since then they
had lived in the hope that some day they would be able to
take revenge. But they all confessed that they were utterly
miserable, and asked us to pray for them that they might
have grace to forgive those who had wronged them.

After the women and girls had left, the meeting continued for two and a half hours. There was just one stream of confession to the very end. And all the time the evangelist was kneeling there by the platform, weeping. At the conclusion of the meeting he finally rose to his feet and faced the congregation. His face was drawn and haggard. "My mind is made up," he cried. "I will never rest until I have killed the man who murdered my father."

I thought that that would be the last that I would see him. But when I entered the church next morning there he was standing by the platform, his face shining like the morning. He asked for permission to say a few words before I began my address. Turning to the schoolboys, he said: "Will the boys who confessed last night, and asked for grace to forgive the murderers of their loved ones, please come up here to the front." The nine boys left their seats and went and stood in a row in front of him.

"I listened to your confessions last night, boys," said the evangelist. "I heard you say that you were willing to forgive those who killed your loved ones. Then you heard me, a leader in the Church, declare that I couldn't forgive and that I would not rest until I had taken revenge on the man who murdered my father. When I went home after the service I thought of how the devil would be sure to take advantage of my example and put you boys to ridicule. People would say that you were too young to know your own minds. Then they would point to me as an intelligent man who surely ought to know his own mind, and say 'he doesn't believe in that foolish talk about forgiving one's enemies.' So, lest the devil should mislead you, I have bought these nine hymn books and I am going to present one to each of you, in the hope that every time you open it to praise God from its pages you will recall how that I, an evangelist, received from Him grace to forgive the murderer of my father."

Just then the list containing the names of those upon whom the Christians had planned to take revenge was brought up to the front and torn into bits and the fragments trampled under foot.

A modest tomb-stone in Newchwang marks the resting-place of William C. Burns. It was here that he last laboured for his Lord. It seems that everywhere this great evangelist went, both in the home-land and in China, all with whom he came in contact were brought to a saving knowledge of Christ. Even the heathen carpenter, who made his coffin, was no exception, and was an elder in the Church when I arrived there.

After the Lord had moved so mightily at Mukden, one of the missionaries there said to me: "God has certainly blessed us here, but I am afraid that He won't be able to do anything at Newchwang. Why, the Church there is so dead, it ought to be buried out of sight!" I replied: "You now know the power of God. Just pray that mercy may be shown to Newchwang." At the close of the meetings at Liaoyang I heard the same story. "We praise God," the missionaries said, "for what He has done for us. But really there's no use expecting anything from Newchwang. It's too far gone to be revived." And again I replied: "But you have seen God's power. Why not pray for it?" At Kwangning and Chinchow and Shinminfu it was just the same. Newchwang was too dead for anything. It was past hope.

Mr. Hunter of Kwangning had gone ahead of me to Newchwang to conduct a series of special prayer-meetings. When we met at the dinner-table, shortly after my arrival, I could see that he was bursting with news. "Strange things have been happening here," he cried, his face alight with joy. "Just that day at the prayer-meeting," he said, "a woman, who had denied her Lord in 1900 in order to save her life, had been terribly broken. She had prayed that another opportunity might be given her for her to offer up her life for her Master. A Christian contractor, too, confessed in tears how he had cheated a certain concern out of $200, and vowed that he would pay the money back before the day was out."

The meetings began the following morning. On entering the pulpit, I bowed as usual for a few moments in prayer. When I looked up it seemed to me as if every last man, woman and child in that church was in the throes of judgment. Tears were flowing freely, and all manner of sin was being confessed. What was the explanation? How was one to account for it? This was the church which had been reported to be dead and beyond all hope. And yet, without a word having been spoken, or a hymn sung, or a prayer offered, this remarkable thing had happened. What other explanation can one offer but that it was the Spirit of God working in answer to the prayers of His revived children at Mukden and Liaoyang and elsewhere, who had seen what He could do and in the light of that vision had interceded on behalf of their needy sister-church.

CHAPTER V

REPENTANCE AND CONFESSION IN SHANSI

SHANSI has been well-named the "martyr province of China." In 1900 it was under the rule of that most infamous of governors, Yu Hsien.[1] In his persecution of the Christian Church this man quite outstripped any other Chinese official during that terrible year. In his province alone over one hundred missionaries, besides many native Christians, were done to death.

Some years ago, in Honan, I was talking with an eminent Chinese scholar from Shansi. He seemed very near to the kingdom. "I am convinced," he said, and there were tears in his eyes as he spoke, "that there can be no salvation for us sinners except through the Redeemer, Jesus Christ." He told me that he had been led to look into the Scriptures as a result of the terrible massacre which had taken place in the governor's yamen at Taiyuanfu in 1900. He happened to be in the courtyard, he said, when about sixty missionaries were driven in and herded together, awaiting execution. What impressed him most of all about these people, he declared, was their amazing fearlessness. There was no panic, no crying for mercy. Roman Catholic and Protestant—they waited on death with perfect calmness.

He went on to say that just before the carnage began a golden-haired girl of about thirteen years of age went and stood before the governor. "Why are you planning to kill us?" she asked, her voice carrying to the farthest corner of the courtyard. "Haven't our doctors come from far-off lands to give their lives for your people? Many with hopeless diseases have been healed; some who were blind have received their sight, and health and happiness have been brought into thousands of your homes because

---

[1] Yu Hsien's son later became a Christian.

of what our doctors have done. Is it because of this good that has been done that you are going to kill us?" The governor's head was down. He had nothing to say. There was really nothing he could say. She continued: "Governor, you talk a lot about filial piety. It is your claim, is it not, that among the hundred virtues filial piety takes the highest place. But you have hundreds of young men in this province who are opium sots and gamblers. Can they exercise filial piety? Can they love their parents and obey their will? Our missionaries have come from foreign lands and have preached Jesus to them, and He has saved them and given them power to live rightly and to love and obey their parents. Is it then, perhaps, because of this good that has been done that we are to be killed?"

By this time the governor was writhing. Each word seemed to touch him to the quick. It was far more than a defence, that brave speech, it was a sentence. It was the girl who sat in judgment and the governor stood at the bar. But the drama lasted only for one brief moment. A soldier, standing near the girl, grasped her by the hair, and with one blow of his sword severed her head from her body. That was the signal for the massacre to begin.

"I saw fifty-nine men, women, and children killed that afternoon," went on the scholar. "Even in the very moment of death every face seemed to hold a smile of peace. I saw one lady speaking cheerfully to a little boy who was clinging to her hand. Then her turn came, and her body fell to the yamen floor. But the little fellow, without the sign of a whimper on his face, stood straight upright, still holding fast his mother's hand. Then another blow, and the little mangled corpse lay beside that of the mother. Is it any wonder, therefore, that such marvellous fortitude should have led me to search your Scriptures and to have compelled me to believe that the Bible is in very truth the Word of God?"

In view of the foregoing, one can understand, perhaps, that it was with a feeling almost akin to awe that I came to Taiyuan in the fall of 1908 to lead a series of special meetings. The blood of the martyrs, shed there eight years before, made it sacred ground to me. It was wonderful how mightily the Spirit of God worked in the Church of Taiyuan during those days. So marked was His presence, indeed, that it was quite a common thing to overhear people in the city telling each other that a "new Jesus" had come. Their reason for saying this was that for years many of the professing Christians had been cheating their neighbours and quarrelling with them. Some, indeed, had gone so far as to revile their parents and beat their wives. It seemed that the other Jesus was too old or had lost His power to keep them in order. But this "new Jesus," it appeared, was doing wonderful things. He was making all those old backsliders get up before the whole Church and confess their sins, and afterwards go right back to their heathen neighbours and pay back anything that they owed, and beg the forgiveness of all whom they had wronged. But what was the greatest surprise of all was that they should even go so far as to abase themselves before their wives, asking their pardon for the way in which they had mistreated them. In this way a Revival served to carry conviction to the great mass of people outside the Church, that the Living God had come among His people.

My programme in Shansi had been so arranged as to give me only one day at Hsichow. It hardly seemed possible that any movement worth speaking of would result in so short a time. I had been warned, too, that there were several very serious hindrances in the Hsichow Church. It seemed that the wife of one of the prominent teachers in the mission school was a woman of ungovernable temper. Some time previous to my coming, in one of her fierce bursts of anger, she had gone blind. With her constant quarrelling she was causing trouble right and left. Yet the missionaries knew quite well that if they said anything to her she would go up and down the street, Chinese fashion, proclaiming at the top of her voice all manner of evil things about them. So they chose to leave her strictly alone.

But the most serious difficulty which the missionaries had to face had arisen in connection with the actions of certain Mr. Kuo, who for many years had been one of the most influential members of the Church. During the Boxer uprising of 1900, he had displayed unusual bravery, having done a great deal to comfort and strengthen his fellow-Christians through months of the most bitter persecution. After the Allies had captured Peking and the Empress Dowager had fled west to Sianfu, and the officials everywhere were becoming frightened and beginning to try and undo the wrongs which had been heaped upon the heads of the hapless Christians, this Mr. Kuo was often called to the residence of the local mandarin for the purpose of consultation. He and the mandarin became quite friendly, and sometimes he would be asked to stay for meals, and drink would be pressed upon him. There came occasions when he returned from the yamen hopelessly drunk, hardly able to stagger back to his home. Once, on returning intoxicated from one of these parties, he had almost killed his wife. The missionaries felt at last that it was their duty to remonstrate with Mr. Kuo on the course which he was taking. He had flown into a rage and left the church, taking half the members with him.

Upon my arrival at Hsichow I sent a note to Mr. Kuo, saying how I had heard of his heroism during the Boxer uprising and that I was very anxious to meet him, and that I hoped he would come to the services on the morrow, as that would probably be my only chance to see him. He was pointed out to me at the service on the following morning. In the afternoon he was back again. I spoke that afternoon upon "Take away the stone"—the text having been pressed upon me as I was on my way to Hsichow. Until about halfway through my address Mr. Kuo seemed quite at ease. Then something seemed to touch him and the tears began to trickle down his cheeks and his head went down.

Concluding my address I opened the meeting for prayer. Several responded, but their prayers were the most humdrum and lifeless things I had ever listened to. It was an exceptionally hot day, and most of us were streaming with perspiration. There were an unusually large number of babies in the audience, and it did seem as if every last one of them was crying at the top of its voice. Over in a neighbouring yard a dog was howling as if it were being torn limb from limb. One found it hard to escape the feeling that it was just a little too much to expect that the Holy Spirit should work amid such an environment. Yet all the time, in common with the other missionaries, I was inwardly praying that somehow His power would be made manifest that afternoon.

Presently Mr. Kuo began to pray. Immediately all the babies seemed to go to sleep. The dog had either escaped or been put out of its misery. And somehow we forgot about the heat. As he went on, in broken accents, confessing his sin, there was the stillness of death in the assembly. As he finished, suppressed sobbing could be heard everywhere. In a little while a woman in the rear of the building started to pray. Her wan, tear-stained face showed plainly that the depths of her heart, too, had been plumbed. Brokenly she confessed to her wicked temper and the way in which God's work had been hindered by it. It was the teacher's wife.

After the service Mr. Kuo and I walked down the street together. "Do you know," he said to me, "I simply can't account for what happened to me this afternoon. All of a sudden I seemed to experience an awful burning inside of me. I felt that I would burn up if I did not confess my sins right there and then and get right with God" . . . *"Is not my word like as a fire? saith the Lord; and like a hammer that breaketh the rock in pieces?"* (Jer. xxiii:29).

When I arrived at Chuwuhsien it was to find that missionaries and Chinese leaders had assembled from three different provinces. Twenty-one stations in all were represented. Every one seemed eager, expectant. Miss Stelman, the senior missionary at Chuwu, said to me: "We have prayed dry for revival here. If God doesn't send revival this time then I don't see how it will be possible for us to continue in prayer. We have exhausted every prayer promise in His Book." I was unavoidably limited to only four days. However, we all laid the matter before the Lord and prayed that He would do a quick work.

My opening address was on "What the Lord has done for His people at Chinchow, Manchuria." I had not been speaking very long before the tears were running down many faces, and heads were bowed in conviction. During the open session for prayer, which followed my address, every one who prayed broke down. The movement, thus begun, continued meeting by meeting throughout the four days. All manner of sin was confessed and put away. The county magistrate, his curiosity aroused by the reports which had been brought to him, came to one meeting dressed in civilian garb and listened to confessions of murder, theft and crime of every description. His amazement knew no bounds, because, as he afterwards said, he would have had to beat those same people almost to death before they would come out with such confessions before him.

Sometimes, although a meeting perhaps had lasted for three hours or more, the people would go right back to their rooms, shut themselves in and continue in prayer. One could go through the compound away on late at night and find little groups here and there engaged in prayer. Long before daylight it was the same.

In the earnestness and importunity of their prayers the Chuwu people reminded me of the Koreans whom I had listened to at Pingyang. One day a former elder, who had been dismissed from the Church not long before, was brought to the meeting. When the Chinese authorities were paying indemnity to the Christians for the losses they had suffered at the hands of the Boxers, this man declared that he had been robbed of 5,000 teals' worth of property. A deacon, who knew him well, said that at the very outside he had not lost more than 100 teals' worth. The magistrate granted him 1,500 teals compensation. From then on he lost ground rapidly. When I arrived at Chuwu he was an opium sot, as was also his wife.

At this meeting, which the ex-elder attended, one Christian after another prayed in tears for his return. They were quite the most moving prayers that I had ever listened to. I did not see how the man could help but yield. But suddenly he got up, uttered some vile curses, and left the church in a rage. That was the last I ever heard of him.

After I left Chuwu the principal of the Boys' School, a man who had been greatly influenced during those days, adopted the practice of getting up for prayer every morning long before dawn and then at daybreak having the boys join in with him. This continued for some twenty days, until finally one morning the Spirit was poured out upon them. Quarrels were made up. Stolen things were returned to their owners. One boy had cruelly beaten a neighbour's dog, and there was nothing else for it but that he should go to the neighbour, and confess his fault. Another had stolen a neighbour's chicken. So he had to go to the neighbour, confess what he had done and repay him.

While I was at Chuwu the Girls' School had not yet opened after the summer holidays. The teachers, however, were at the meetings and were among those who were most deeply moved. When the girls returned, the teachers told them in the prayer-meeting morning by morning about what God had been doing. The girls pressed for a day of fasting and prayer that they, too, might receive the blessing. The teachers brought the matter before Miss Stelman, who said: "Just wait a day or two and we'll pray about it." The following morning, when the girls were assembled for prayer, the Spirit fell upon them, and I understand that it was late in the afternoon before they finally got up from their knees.

It was at Hungtunghsien that the famous Pastor Hsi ministered so faithfully and with such splendid results for many years. After Pastor Hsi's death a certain Elder Hsu was appointed to fill his position. The new pastor was a man of advanced ideas. He aimed to make his

church renowned throughout the province. There were to be
no poor among its members. To the farmers he said:
"The Lord has given you splendid land. My suggestion
is that you stop growing wheat. There's scarcely any
money in that. Grow opium instead. Of course, being
Christians, you won't smoke opium. But since there's a
demand for it why not supply it? Besides, if you grow
opium, you will have all the more money to make our
church flourish."

What a man sows that he will also reap. The people
followed their pastor's advice, with the inevitable result
that in a few years many of them had become opium ad-
dicts. But that was not all. At Pastor Hsu's direction the
church established a large cash shop in the city. For a
time it flourished. Then the leaders became more covetous and issued bogus money. The bank went smash,
and the reputation of the church or what was left of it
went down with it. With this last disgrace the patience
of the missionaries was exhausted. Pastor Hsu was dismissed and all opium sots were cut off from the church.

During the few days that I was at Hungtung the Spirit
of Burning was very much in evidence. Hidden sins were
continually being brought out. One day, while the people
were praying and a profound spiritual atmosphere seemed
to fill the church, a missionary sitting by me whispered
that the ex-pastor had just come in. From the moment
that the man entered the building all sense of God's presence seemed to depart. The very devil appeared to take
control of the meeting. This lasted for almost half an
hour. Then he went out, and immediately men and women
everywhere began to break down under conviction of
sin, and the sense of God's nearness returned.

I quote this as a striking instance of the power of
hindrance in an unrepentant leader. Not long afterwards,
the ex-pastor had Buddhist and Taoist priests attend his
father's burial and had it published around the province
that he had been fooled by the missionaries and that there
was nothing in Christianity.

CHAPTER VI

AN OUTPOURING OF DIVINE BLESSING
UPON CHANGTEHFU

ONE can appreciate how it must have been with a peculiarly keen sense of anticipation that I returned to my own home station after my visit to Korea in the summer of 1907. On the Sunday morning that I told the story of the Revival the Chinese leaders crowded around me after the service insisting that I immediately give them a week of special meetings. The matter was broached to the other missionaries at the station. Yes, we might have the meetings if we wished. But the general routine was to be interfered with as little as possible. Certainly, the schools were not to be closed in order to allow the pupils to attend the meetings. The warm support accorded me by the Chinese leaders, however, more than made up for any indifference in other quarters. I often look back to those wonderful days I had with them.

The meetings ended on a Saturday. Next day I addressed the whole congregation at the usual Sunday morning service. From the very first I felt as though I were talking against a stone wall. About halfway through my address I said: "The Spirit of God is being hindered. It is no use for me to go on speaking. Will several brethren pray?" Several prayers were offered, but they were of a very ordinary nature and clearly without spiritual power. "Stop!" I cried. "Plainly there is some one in this audience who is hindering God." I pronounced the benediction and the meeting broke up.

During the months that followed a marked change took place in the attitude of my brother missionaries. Certainly it was no longer possible to blind one's eyes to the fact that the spiritual condition of the station had reached a very low ebb. The Boys' School, especially, was causing no little anxiety. It was being found almost

impossible to maintain any semblance of discipline. Some
of the senior students had run away. Others were secretly planning to follow their example. Finally, the missionaries had come to the conclusion that unless something happened to change the temper of the boys, the
school had better be closed. It was in the spring of 1908
that the invitation was extended to me to conduct a ten
days' series of meetings, full support being promised me.

In Manchuria and elsewhere the question had sometimes been put to me: "Do you believe that you will meet
with the same manifestations of the Spirit's power in
Honan, where your faults and weaknesses are known, as
in these places where you are a comparative stranger?"
It was a difficult question. As the time drew near for the
start of the Changtehfu meetings I became decidedly uneasy. Early on the morning of the first meeting I was
pacing restlessly up and down my room, my mind in a
turmoil. I had often heard of people going to the Bible,
opening it at random, and finding some text seemingly
written for their own immediate need; but this had never
been my custom. Yet this morning I felt, as perhaps
never before, the need of Divine light to strengthen my
wavering faith.

As I took up my Bible it seemed to open of itself. My
eye was arrested by these words: "From the rising of the
sun even unto the going down of the same, my name shall
be great among the Gentiles" (Mal. i. 11). It was an
answer clearly enough; and my faith was restored. Yet
in a little while a doubt began to arise. There was, of
course, no question, a voice seemed to say, that the text
included Honan. But wasn't it stretching the point a little
to take it that it referred even to my own station of
Changteh? Once again I took up my Bible. Strangely
enough, it opened at the same place. This time my eye
caught the words, following immediately after those
which I have already quoted—*"And in every place . . ."*
That means this station, I said to myself. Somehow I
knew then that God was going to move Changteh.

The missionaries had been most praiseworthy in the preparations which they had made for the meetings. As for the Chinese leaders they were, if possible, even more whole-hearted in their support than they had been before. Feeling that the church, which had a seating capacity of only six hundred, was too small, they had on their own initiative erected in the adjoining yard a large mat pavilion. Christians had come in for the services from all parts of the field. The schools had been closed, and even in the hospital arrangements had been made to allow as many of the staff as possible to attend the meetings. Visiting missionaries and Chinese leaders were there; some having come long distances.

From the very first it seemed as if God had marked out Changteh for a special outpouring of Divine blessing. On the morning of the second day a number broke down and confessed their sins. Among these was a Mr. Fan, who was a noted scholar and a teacher in the Girls' School. That evening, at the missionary prayer-meeting, two lady missionaries, who for a long time had not been on speaking terms with each other, asked each other's forgiveness and made up their quarrel. At that same meeting the principal of the Girls' School confessed to the sins which she felt were hindering God's work. As we were passing the Girls' School, on our way to the evening service, the sound that reached us made it seem as if all the girls were praying and confessing at the same time.

All through the third and fourth days there was a deepening sense of God's presence. Mr. Hu, one of our leading evangelists, had been asked to lead the general prayer-meeting on the evening of the fourth day. On rising to open the meeting he said: "I must confess my own sins before I attempt to lead this meeting. When the reports of the Manchurian Revival began to reach us, I said to the other evangelists, 'This is not the Holy Spirit's work. It is just Mr. Goforth's way of manipulating an audience by a sort of mesmeric power. I assure you that when he comes to Changteh he will run up against Hu Feng Hua, a man who has a resolution and mind of his own. Hypnotism won't be able to affect him.'

"On the second morning." he continued, "when I saw teacher Fan, a B.A. from my own village, down in the dust, weeping like a little child and confessing his sins, I was more than disgusted. I assured myself that this could not possibly be the Spirit of God. It was just toadying to the foreigner. As the day progressed, I became more and more scornful at the way things were going. What weak creatures they must be, I thought, to give way as they were doing!

"On the third day, as the movement increased in intensity and the people seemed to be swept along in spite of themselves, I became a little uneasy. Gradually the thought began to take shape in my mind, 'Can it be that I am mistaken? What if it should turn out that I am actually opposing God?' Last night I hardly slept a wink, and this morning I was like a man demented. Instead of going to the meeting, I wandered out through the fields, not knowing where I was going. The torment in my mind became ever more agonizing. I came back and went into the evangelists' room. Evangelist Cheng was there. 'What's wrong with me?' I asked. 'Am I going mad?' 'No,' replied Evangelist Cheng, 'I don't believe you're going mad. Just kneel down there and you will soon find out what the trouble is.' While he was praying my heart was broken and I sobbed like a little child. I knew then that I had been pitting myself against God the Holy Spirit."

I had prayerfully hoped that, after such a confession, great things would result. But, to my keen disappointment, it was an insignificant church member, and one whose life had been anything but straight, who rose to pray. It was not long, however, before it became evident that God had chosen this humble vessel to do His work that evening. (In the afternoon, although I had not believed it at the time, the man had gone through a terrible shaking-up and had made a most broken confession). He was weeping now. He seemed to have caught a vision of the Savior. "What, Lord!" he cried, "You standing there outside the door, patiently knocking! That should not be. The temple is Thy purchased possession. You have given Your life to redeem it. If You are outside the door, then there must be some one inside who is preferred before You." He went on in that strain for several minutes; and, as he prayed, different ones all over the audience broke down in an agony of conviction. Never have I listened to a prayer that seemed more genuinely inspired.

Suddenly, to my great disappointment, he stopped and sat down. I felt certain that he hadn't finished his work. Ten minutes went by and then he rose again. It was the same vision, but now his whole being seemed enthralled. "What, Lord!" he cried, "You waiting there still? You, who art Lord of all! One word from You would sweep us sinners from the earth. Is it possible that still we defy You and bar You from Your own temple?" At these words the whole audience gave way and melted like wax.

To show how carefully even the most favored must walk in the presence of the Lord, I will mention an incident which occurred on the following evening. Shortly after the meeting had been thrown open for prayer, I heard a peculiar moaning sound. Looking up I saw this man, who had been so wonderfully used the evening before, groaning horribly and going through all manner of rhythmical movements. Suddenly, as I was watching him, he threw himself full length upon the ground. It was clear enough that the devil had got hold of him. Realizing what a powerful effect his prayer had produced the night before, he had probably decided that this time he was going to stage something really extraordinary. Although I disliked intensely to interfere, I was afraid that, if I left him alone, he would soon have imitators. I went down and gave him a sharp slap on the side, saying, "Get up and pray decently." He stopped on the instant, and shamefacedly slunk into his seat.

On the fifth day so many were moved to prayer and confession that I had barely time to give my addresses.

One of the most startling confessions of that day was from the principal of the Boys' School. He was a man whom we had all along thought was almost perfect. Yet before that great audience, including his own pupils, he gave one of the humblest and most heart-searching confessions that I have ever listened to. Before nightfall the revival fire had swept through his school.

As the meetings went on many of those who had received a blessing hastened back to their villages, and urged their relatives and friends to return with them at once to Changteh, saying that "the Spirit of God has come." Others, who would not get away, hired messengers to go to their home places and bring back their families. On the seventh day the movement became so powerful that I did not have a chance to give either a forenoon or an afternoon address. In fact, from then on till the end of the meetings there were so many anxious to confess, that it was usually found impossible to limit a meeting to less than three hours.

On the seventh evening, Dr. L—— came up on the platform and asked for an opportunity to say a few words. Addressing the congregation, he said: "From the beginning of this movement, with which Mr. Goforth has been connected, I have refused to believe that it originated with, or was guided by, the Holy Spirit. The conclusion that I arrived at was that it was due to some hypnotic power which Mr. Goforth was able to exercise over his audiences. But what I have seen here these past few days has convinced me, even against my will, that I was wrong. I was attributing to a man what only God could bring about. I want to say now that I believe, with all my heart, that this movement is truly of the Spirit of God." Whereupon he turned to me, before everyone, and asked me to forgive him. Then, addressing the people again, he said: "I also want to ask your forgiveness. I have done you an injury in imagining that you could be moved, as you have been these days, by any other agency but the Divine."

Word of what was happening at Changteh having gone around the country, fresh bands of Christians from all parts of the field were constantly arriving. Many of the newcomers were brought under conviction before they had scarcely entered the compound. Sometimes people would be praying in their rooms, hours before a meeting opened. Then, when the time came, they would go and pour out their confessions.

Again, on the eighth day, I found it impossible to give an address. At the morning meeting even the schoolboys were getting up on their benches, and in tears confessing to all manner of sin. This was too much for Dr. M——. At the conclusion of the meeting, he declared: "After what I have heard this morning it is impossible for me to take any further part in the meetings. It couldn't have been anything else than the devil which got into those boys. How could they know anything about the things of which they professed themselves guilty? They had listened to the confessions of the grown-ups and they were simply playing the parrot." "Better be careful, Doctor," I said, "about judging too hastily. After all, how are we to determine the depth of iniquity which may lie even in a schoolboy's heart?"

Dr. M—— had been appointed to take charge of the afternoon meeting. It was only after much persuasion that we induced him to fill the position. That afternoon one after another of his own and other evangelists told how their hearts had been cut to the quick at the schoolboys' confessions. "Well, this has certainly been a great revelation to me," said Dr. M—— after the meeting. "Never again will I make out that I know what is the moving of the Spirit of God."

The original plan had been that the meetings should last for eight days; but when the eighth day came every one was agreed that we should go on for several days longer. During these last days a number, who had held out up till then, felt that things were becoming too hot for them and tried to run away. But they found out what a difficult thing it is to escape from a seeking God. Some only got part way home, when the pressure became so unbearable that they had to turn around and come back. Others got all the way home, but, finding no relief, they returned to Changteh.

One wealthy man, to whom the idea of public confession was particularly distasteful, had got a few miles from the city when he realised that it was useless for him to go any farther. He came back, and standing up in the rear of the tent, with the tears coursing down his cheeks, he cried out to me: "Pastor, do I have to wait until all those up there at the front have got through?" I replied that since they had got there first it was only fair that we should hear them first. "But, Pastor," he said, "I can't wait. I'll burst if I'm not given a chance to confess my sin right away." "Well, if that's the case," I said, "I think we had better hear you now; and the others will have to be patient." Then followed the confession—coming like a torrent, bursting through the dam which had tried to hold it in check.

Often, during the meetings, great waves of prayer would sweep the congregation. Some one would cry, "Oh, do pray for my out-station; we're so cold and dead out there." Or another would tell of how his father and mother were unconverted, and plead with the people to join him in prayer for them. Instantly scores all over the audience would respond. It seemed that nothing could resist such importunity. A number of our most influential Chinese leaders had been opposed to the meetings and had declared beforehand that they had not the slightest intention of attending them. Special intercession was offered up on behalf of these men; and as I remember, some of the most broken confessions of the whole movement were from them.

All kinds of quarrels were made up and innumerable wrongs righted during those days. Though many confessed to the grosser sins, yet the burden of perhaps the majority ran along the line of neglected duty. The Sabbath question, tithing, testimony to others, right example, neglect of the Bible, believing prayer for their loved ones and friends—these were the matters concerning which many in great brokenness confessed their failure.

It was remarkable, too, how even the outsiders, who came into the compound merely out of curiosity, were often brought under conviction. With many it seemed that an irresistible pressure drew them to the tent to confess their sins and acknowledge Christ as Savior. There was one young man in the hospital who had had both his legs cut off by a train. From his room in the ward it was quite impossible for the man to hear my voice. Yet during one of the meetings, when the movement in the tent was at its height, he came under conviction of sin and was converted.

But any account of the movement at Changteh would be incomplete if it did not contain the story of how God dealt with my old friend, Wang Ee, of Takwanchwang, a village some twenty-five li southeast of our station. Wang Ee was one of our strongest converts. My home had no more frequent nor more welcome visitor than he. For a number of years after his conversion the Lord's cause prospered greatly in his village. Some notorious sinners were saved, and by 1900 there were altogether nineteen families in the village professing Christ. In Wang Ee's own household, out of twenty-eight members, all save two had become Christians.

In 1900 the Boxer trouble broke out. The Chinese leaders immediately urged us to flee, while there was time. They assured us that, if we stayed, probably all, missionaries and Chinese Christians alike, would be massacred. If, on the other hand, we managed to get to a place of safety, we could remain there until the storm had blown over and then return. This is not the place to tell of the harrowing experiences through which we passed before we finally reached the safety of the coast. The Christians in Honan, and among them my friends at Takwanchwang, went through great persecution and were stripped of practically everything.

On my return to Changteh, in the spring of 1902, I immediately hurried out to Takwanchwang. What a meeting that was! We all gathered in Wang Ee's home, and they showed me their scars and I showed them mine. Then we all knelt down and praised God for His mercy to us. Destitute as they were, not one of the little band had been killed. I felt that surely, since God had brought His people safely through such trials, He must have great things in store for them.

Shortly after this visit, I entered upon the evangelisation of the northern portion of the field, and another missionary took over the southern section in which Takwanchwang was situated. Thus, for a number of years, I was not able to visit the station again. Wang Ee, however, often came to call on me. When I would ask him how the work was prospering in Takwanchwang his face would fall and he would reply: "Not very well, I am afraid. But, Pastor, you mustn't blame me. God's time hasn't come yet. When His time comes He will save the people of my village." Somehow I felt that the hindrance must be with my friend, but where or how I had no means of determining.

In the fall of 1908 I wrote a letter to Wang Ee asking him, as a special favor to myself, to come and attend the meetings which were to be held at Changteh. But at the opening meeting I looked in vain for the familiar face of my old friend. His son, however, had come. I said to the young man: "I sent especially for your father. Why didn't he come?" He replied: "My father sent me in his stead. He says that he is old and will soon pass on, and that he wants me to learn all I can so as to be able to take his place in the church after he has gone." On the third day the young fellow appeared to be greatly moved. "You go home," I said to him, "and tell your father that he simply must come; and that if he doesn't he will offend his best friend."

Next morning Wang Ee turned up. His greeting was cold. "Why did you send my son home?" he asked resentfully; "he would have got far more out of these meetings than I could. There is really no particular reason why I should come. I haven't any sin." "Wang Ee," I said, "I just want to ask one thing of you; and that is that you should stay here several days and just see if God has anything to say to you."

On the sixth morning, before breakfast, Evangelist Ho came to my home in great excitement. "Wang Ee is in a terrible state," he said. "Late last night, as he was talking with some of us evangelists, he suddenly fell down on the floor as if he had been shot. Ever since he has been weeping and crying out about his sin. He has sent me to ask you to start the meeting as soon as possible so that he can have a chance to make his confession."

As soon as breakfast was over, I hurried out to the yard. Just outside the door of the tent I met Wang Ee. The tears were streaming down his cheeks. He was so overcome that he could not say a word. He just grasped my arm. This was too much for me, and I found I couldn't keep the tears back myself. Arm in arm we entered the tent. Wang Ee knelt down on the platform. For a few minutes the great sobs that shook his frame rendered him speechless. But at last, finding his voice, he cried: "I told Pastor Goforth that the people of Tagwanchwang had not been saved because God's time was not up. I lied to him. It was because Wang Ee's time was not up. I have sinned and grieved the Holy Spirit. After 1900, when the official was compelled to indemnify me for the property which had been stolen or destroyed by the Boxers, I grossly exaggerated my losses. Where I had only lost three mules I made out a claim for six and got paid for six. Where I had been robbed of three hundred bushels of wheat I declared that I had been robbed of six hundred, and I was paid for six hundred. By lying in this way I have been made rich out of adversity and quenched the Holy Spirit in my heart."

Wang Ee concluded with the declaration that he would use every cent, which he had got dishonestly from the Boxer Indemnity, in the construction of a church in his native village. And he kept his word.

Chapter VII

THE LORD'S PRESENCE AND POWER IN THE CHANGTEHFU OUT-STATIONS

AFTER the Changtehfu meetings the missionaries and Chinese leaders formed themselves into bands and toured the various out-stations. Among those visited was a certain village where, not long before, over a hundred of our Christians had gone over to the Church of Rome. The trouble had arisen over a law-suit. A certain notorious character in the village had suddenly surprised every one by professing Christ. For six months he had continued to walk the way of a Christian, and then finally had turned again to his sin and was arrested for robbery. The elders and deacons of the church had come to us, begging us to interfere. They assured us that all we needed to do, in order to save the man's life, would be to tell the magistrate that he was an earnest Christian and that he must have been wrongfully arrested. We refused to perjure ourselves to save him. They left us and went straight over to the Roman Catholic priest. He named his price. He would save the man on condition that they should all join the Church of Rome. They gave the promise; the priest immediately got in touch with the mandarin, and a few hours later the man was set free. Practically the whole Church went over to Rome, just a remnant remaining faithful.

During the Revival at Changteh this out-station was the burden of many a prayer. Sometimes there would be hundreds at a time imploring God to bring the lost ones back to the fold. A deputation was sent out to the village, and they practically dragged the chief elder and the chief deacon back with them. Both men were brought under terrible conviction. Not long afterwards Dr. M——, at the head of a band of revived Chinese leaders, went to the village to conduct four days of special meetings. Dr.

M—— assured me afterwards that he had never listened to people so apparently under the spirit of judgment. Over a hundred made public confession; and the whole Church turned back from Rome.

Dr. M—— and his band went on to Changtsun. Unusual interest was manifested in the meetings. One day as many as five thousand people gathered to listen. It was found necessary to erect platforms at different strategic points in order that all might be reached. Years later, after the Church at Changtsun had been organized, I was invited there to lead in a series of revival meetings. The church being considered too small, the meetings were held out in a large open yard near-by. For several days there was absolutely no evidence of any spiritual movement. There seemed to be some unaccountable hindrance.

On the third morning Mrs. Goforth said to me: "This is getting on my nerves. I can't stay here any longer. I wasn't present at that first meeting, but judging from little things that have been dropped you must have mortally offended the people by something you said. Why, I've never seen people act like this. You give your address, then announce that the meeting is open for prayer. You wait for ten minutes with no result, every one being as dumb as a post. Then you have them sing a hymn, after which you again open the meeting for prayer. Another long interval passes, but still not a word from any one. Then you pronounce the benediction. This has been going on for days. I can't stand it."

"I don't know how I could have offended them," I replied. "All I remember saying, at that first meeting, was that if they had any old prayers which they had learnt off by heart I would be glad if they would lay them on the shelf until these meetings were over. But I told them that if the Spirit of God prompted them to get rid of different things which they had reason to believe were hindering His cause in this place, then we would be only too glad to hear that kind of praying."

As we were talking my diary lay open on the table in front of me. I had just been writing a note in it. "Just read this," I said, handing the book to my wife. "This is the third day, with not the slightest sign of any spiritual awakening among the people. But, as surely as God is omnipotent and His Word like a hammer that breaks the rock in pieces, so surely shall His people bend into the very dust before Him." Mrs. Goforth handed the diary back to me. "I won't go home," she said. "I'll wait and see what God is going to do." Just then the Chinese pastor was ushered in. He was greatly worked up over the fact of there being as yet no sign of Revival, and he told us that the leaders felt so keenly about the matter that they had that morning started an extra prayer-meeting.

From then on our one difficulty was to get the meetings closed. Sometimes after a meeting had lasted for three or four hours I would pronounce the benediction, and immediately dozens would come running up to the platform, pleading with me to give them a chance to confess. Each day the unconverted came in larger numbers, and many were brought under conviction. One Christian said to me: "Before these meetings there was no special interest in the Gospel in my village. But today, when I went home for my noon-meal, about ninety of my fellow-villagers gathered around me and asked me to tell them all about 'this Jesus and His way of salvation'." Among the new converts were two noted witches. They had Pastor Hsi and the elders go back with them to their homes to hold a service. All in their families turned to the Lord.

Even among the Christian leaders the brokenness and conviction were startling. Pastor and elders and deacons all besought God to forgive them for the coldness and laxity of their Christian service. Many prayed earnestly for a deeper experience of the spirit of brotherly love. Others in shame confessed how they hadn't read their Bibles, how they hadn't prayed, how they had not made any attempt to save those around them.

Sometimes, when people ask: "What about permanent results?" I tell them the story of Kuo Lao Tsui. Kuo lived in a little village about five miles from Changtsun. He had once been one of the wealthiest men in the district, but had become addicted to opium, and in a short time had squandered almost everything. His condition was such that even the weight of a quilt on him was agony to him. He couldn't sleep a wink unless dosed full of opium. His wife finally died of a broken heart, leaving one little child. Kuo had immediately taken to himself another wife, a young woman in her teens who had been forced into the marriage by her family. It is said that when the poor girl had correctly sized up the situation she fell into a fit of weeping that lasted for days; for she knew quite well that this husband who had been forced upon her might die off at any moment; and that would mean that both she and the child would be sold into slavery.

During the Revival at Changtsun a number from Kuo's village attended the meetings, and were brought under conviction. One day four of the new converts called at Kuo's house and told him to get ready as they would be back in half an hour to take him to Changtsun "to get saved." When the men returned the first thing they did was to destroy Kuo's opium pipe and pitch his opium into the fire. Kuo had had a suspicion that they would do this, so he had secreted some morphia pills in the lining of his garment. It was his intention that, when the craving came on him with its irresistible power, he would first make sure that no one was looking and then just take one of these pills out and eat it. But his friends were up to his tricks. They searched his garment, removed all the pills and threw them into the fire, too.

Poor Kuo was now in a terrible state. "What am I going to do?" he groaned; "I can't live without it." "We'll pray for you," his friends replied. As Kuo couldn't even bear the jolting of a cart, the men set him in a big animal feed-basket, and the four of them carried him the five miles into the meeting. To his great surprise, Kuo slept all through the first night without any uneasiness. As yet, however, it did not occur to him to give God the credit. He decided that it was probably due to the fact that the extra dose of opium, which he had taken as a precautionary measure prior to setting out on the journey, had not as yet worked off its effects. The second night, as he was about to retire, an intolerable craving came over him. His friends, seeing his distress, walked him around the village several times, brought him back to his room, prayed with him, then put him to bed. He slept peacefully all through that night. In five days the craving had completely disappeared, and Kuo was a new man in Christ Jesus.

In a few years Kuo came to be recognized as one of the ablest preachers in North Honan. He set to work, too, and recovered all the property which he had lost. On one occasion I heard him give his testimony before a large crowd which had gathered from his own and neighbouring villages. "You people know what a hopeless wreck I was at forty-five years of age," he said. "I had squandered away all I possessed. My first wife had died of a broken heart. My second wife was living in a continuous agony of apprehension. She expected me to die off any day. In those days I couldn't walk five li to save my life. Now I'm sixty years of age and I can walk ninety li any day without the slightest difficulty. I have a happy wife and four happy children. My two eldest daughters are graduates of the Christian Girls' School at Changteh. My youngest son and daughter are at present attending the same school. Yes, I can certainly recommend my Savior, the Lord Jesus Christ, for He has surely done great things for me."

In that same district there was a farmer by the name of Yeh. Early in the fall of 1908 Yeh became involved in a law-suit with a certain Mr. Chang, who lived in the town of Changtsun. The Changs were a well-to-do scholarly family, with considerable influence in the neighbourhood; while Yeh was only a poor, insignificant peasant. The Changs won the case. Yeh, burning with a sense of injustice, went up to the higher courts at Changteh to have the case retried. As he was passing through the city he encountered a Christian from his native village, who, on learning of his business in Changteh, persuaded him to put it off for a day and come with him to the mission. It was during the Revival. I happened to be preaching that day on the text, "But if ye forgive not men their trespasses, neither will your Father forgive your trespasses" (Matt. vi. 15).

Yeh was mightily convicted, and resolved then and there that he would become a Christian. All thought of going to law with the Changs passed from his mind. He wondered instead what he might do to lead them to Christ. The difference in their social levels, which rendered opportunities for contact of remote possibility, constituted the chief difficulty. It happened, however, that, shortly after his return home, Yeh was passing one day in front of the Chang house when Mr. Chang himself came out. Yeh bowed courteously and asked after his health. The old scholar glanced at him with supreme contempt, then turned away without saying a word. Such a rebuff was enough to dishearten any man—but not Yeh. After that, whenever he met one of the Chang family on the street, he would go out of his way to be friendly with him.

Gradually old Mr. Chang began to soften. For a long time the family could think of no explanation to offer for Yeh's sudden change of attitude. He had gone up to Changtehfu threatening all manner of revenge, and then a few days later had returned and had thereafter manifested only the friendliest and most lovable spirit towards them. What could have happened? They wondered. Then one day a member of the family came back with the news that, while Yeh was at Changteh, he had gone over to the place where the "foreign devils" lived in the north suburb, and had decided to become a Christian. Whether that provided the solution of the mystery or not, they did not know. The fact remained that Yeh was plainly desirous of letting bygones be bygones. They finally decided to meet him half-way. Three months later Yeh had won the whole Chang family to Christ.

I wish to mention just one other incident before concluding this chapter. For a number of years the condition of the Church at Linchang, which was one of our largest out-stations, situated about thirty miles north-east of Changtehfu, had been anything but encouraging. I finally decided to give it a week of special meetings. We had good reason to believe that the unsatisfactory condition of the Church was largely due to the wrong living of one of the deacons. Nothing definite, however, could be fastened on the deacon. He was a wily customer, and always managed to cover up his tracks. On the Sunday morning that the meetings opened, I approached the deacon and urged him to stay for the whole series, pointing out how valuable his assistance would be to us. He made no reply, but immediately headed for his home, which was about twenty-two li away.

Monday came and there was no deacon. Tuesday—and still he had not put in an appearance. Elder Chang became so wrought up about the matter that he set out early on Wednesday morning and brought the deacon back with him. At the close of the forenoon service I said to him: "Now, deacon, you have remained away two days. Won't you please stay with us till the end of the services?" He simply mumbled something incoherent and left me. Elder Chang did his best to get him to stay, but was met with the scornful reply: "Do you suppose that I could demean myself and confess my sins like those people did this morning? Why, I would die first."

Later, I saw the deacon and the elder out across the ploughed fields, the deacon struggling to get away and the elder trying to hold him back. Finally, the elder gave it up and came back, weeping, to the room where Mrs. Goforth and I were staying. He was very discouraged. I suggested that the three of us should unite in prayer for the deacon. "His case is not beyond God's power," I said. "Remember what Christ said, that 'if two of you shall agree on earth as touching anything that they shall ask, it shall be done for them of My Father which is in heaven'" (Matt. xviii. 19). As we knelt in silent prayer,

I cried, "O Lord, Thou canst see that this deacon won't stay at the meeting and thus give Thee a chance to bring him to a consciousness of his sin. Yet, even in his own home make him realize that he is the most miserable man in this country today. Don't let him sleep a wink tonight. Give him the consciousness that he is passing through hell; and bring him back on the morrow to glorify his Savior."

Early next morning the deacon turned up. He was the picture of misery. "I've passed through hell since I left here yesterday," he moaned. "I couldn't sleep last night. I'm sure that I'm the most unhappy man in China today."

When the deacon came up on the platform that morning to make his confession he was so overcome with emotion that he was scarcely able to speak. He took his stand by the blackboard. "My sins are too great," he cried, "for me to confess them simply by word of mouth. I must write them down." In large, clear characters he wrote, "LIAR." Then, turning to the audience, he said, "Yes, I'm a liar. I've lied to God the Holy Spirit. When He moved me at the great Revival at Changtehfu I vowed that in everything I would endeavor to live as became a leader in His Church. Instead, I have served the devil. I'm a liar." He turned to the blackboard again, and wrote "ADULTERER." Then "MURDERER." "Another man and I," he said, "planned to waylay a wealthy business man. We were going to kill him and then take his money. We waited by the roadside in the dark for hours; but our intended victim decided, almost at the last moment, not to leave the city that night. Nevertheless, I'm a murderer at heart."

It is impossible to put in words the effect that was produced by that remarkable confession. It seemed to be the one thing needed to allow the Spirit of God full power over the people's hearts.

CHAPTER VIII

EVIL SPIRITS DEFEATED AND CAST OUT IN HONAN

I WAS asked to hold meetings at Kaifeng on two different occasions. The first time I was faced with some unaccountable hindrance right up till the last day of the services. Different ones were brought under conviction, but there was nothing like the free movement of the Spirit which I had seen in Manchuria and at Changteh. During the final meeting, though, one of the medical assistants, a Mr. Kao, cried out to a colleague, "God is being held up here because of us. We are at enmity with each other and every one knows it. Let us get rid of this hindrance." The other immediately stood up and confessed his part in the quarrel. Whereupon the whole audience broke down. There were a large number of outsiders present that evening, and they especially seemed to be affected. I went around amongst them and heard many yielding outright and crying for mercy.[1]

On the occasion of my second visit to Kaifeng the meetings were conducted especially for the students of Mr. Salee's school. There were about 140 students in the school, of whom perhaps 20 per cent were Christians. During the eight days that I was with the boys no real movement became evident. As a matter of fact, they did not have a fair chance. Japan had just brought in her "Twenty-one Demands," and naturally every one was wrought up to the highest pitch. The day on which our meetings opened a big public gathering was held in the city, the students, as usual, being very much in evidence. Speakers were chosen, who denounced the Japanese in the most violent terms and insisted that steps should be taken to wipe out this national disgrace. A number of students from the Government schools, both male and fe-

[1] Since then Mr. Kao has been greatly used in the opening up of new mission work in Kansu province.

male, let out their own blood and inscribed vows of undying hatred against Japan.

On the fourth day of the meetings a note was sent to Mr. Salee's students from the girls of one of the Government schools in the city. The note ran something like this: "We thought you were men, and that you would naturally take the lead in the defence of your country. But we see now that we were mistaken. You're just a bunch of 'sissies'. We're so disgusted with you that we've decided to send you some girls' clothes to put on." The boys were so aroused that they stationed guards at the gate to ward off any who would approach with suspicious-looking bundles. One can understand, therefore, how the boys were not exactly in a receptive mood for the message which I had come to deliver to them. In fact, Mr. Salee had the greatest difficulty in even keeping the school together at all.

I had to leave Kaifeng directly the meetings were over. Mr. Salee accompanied me to the station. Just before saying good-bye I strongly urged him to continue the meetings, and he promised that he would. He told me afterwards that on his way back to the school he was very much depressed. He kept thinking, he said, "If that man, who has had so much experience, can't do anything, what can I do?" Still, he had promised to go on with the meetings, and he had no intention of going back on his word.

On arriving back at the school, he called the boys together and gave a short address. When he had finished, the head Chinese teacher came up on the platform. For several minutes the man could do nothing but weep. When he was finally able to control himself, he said: "I was smoking cigarettes with some of the students. Mrs. Salee, on hearing about it, called me in and charged me with it. I protested my innocence. 'You know, Mrs. Salee,' I said to her, 'before I became a Christian I was a smoker; but since my conversion I've given it up. And surely, you don't suppose that I, a Christian and a teacher, would go

and smoke cigarettes with the students?' Mrs. Salee
seemed to be satisfied with my explanation; but I wasn't.
That was a year ago, and since then every time I've tried
to pray that lie has come back and stopped me."

A powerful effect, it seems, was produced by this confession. Conviction swept over the students, the non-
Christians as well as the Christians. One of the non-
Christian students, a boy who had been the ring-leader in
every insubordination and devilry, was terribly broken
up and was the first to confess his sins. Many of the boys
followed his example. By the following afternoon as
many as fifty-five of the non-Christian students had gone
to Mr. Salee's study and professed Christ as their Savior.

Here are two clear instances, in one city, of how God
was held up by the sins of His own professed followers.
In both cases, as soon as the sin had been brought to light
and the stone of hindrance removed, the Holy Spirit broke
through in all the fulness of His convicting power. May
we not say that this is a law of God's kingdom? Without
the 120 first being filled with the Holy Spirit it would have
been impossible for those three thousand, on the day of
Pentecost, to have been brought to a saving knowledge
of Jesus Christ.

The work at Kwangchow had been started in the nineties
by Mr. Argento, an Italian. Upon becoming a Christian,
Mr. Argento had been turned out of his home. He joined
the China Inland Mission, and was sent to Kwangchow,
where, in a few years, he had gathered a little band of
Christians around him. Their practice was to get up
before daylight to study the Scriptures together. In 1900
the Boxers bound Mr. Argento, poured kerosene over
him and set him on fire. Some of his friends, however,
came to the rescue and managed to save his life; but his
sight was lost and other parts of his body were badly burnt.
The Mission urged him to go back to Europe, but he would
not think of it. "If I can't see," he said, "I can at least
stay here and pray for the salvation of my people."

But, after a few years, his health became so wretched that he was obliged to leave China for good. He made his home with his wife's people in Norway. A neighbour of Mr. Argento's in Norway told me how the spirit of prayer was constantly upon him. Often he would be up till long after midnight interceding for the people of Kwangchow. Sometimes his wife would say: "You can't stand this; you're too weak. You must go to bed." To this he would reply: "How can I sleep, when so many thousands off there in Kwangchow are dying without Jesus?"

When I arrived at Kwangchow in December, 1915, I saw the last tile being put in its place on the roof of a fine church. The church was pointed out to me as an example of the fruit of Mr. Argento's sacrificial ministry. It possessed seating capacity for 1,400 people, and had been built entirely out of funds contributed by Chinese Christians. At that time there were two thousand Christians in the city of Kwangchow and throughout the surrounding country. There were, besides, twenty-one outstations, and of all the workers only two were being paid out of foreign funds.

Shortly after my arrival, I was introduced to Elder Wen. In accordance with Chinese custom, I asked the elder how old he was. With a twinkle in his eye he replied, "I'm just eighteen years old." He had grey hair, and I had guessed that he must be at least sixty. "It is true," he went on to explain, "I am eighteen years old. Before that I was dead in trespasses and sins. I was an opium sot, a drunkard, and a gambler. I had become so weakened by my debauchery that one day a friend of mine, meeting me on the street, looked absolutely aghast at my appearance. 'Look here, Wen,' he said, 'you can't last much longer at the rate you're going. You had better go right over to that Jesus church and have the missionary pray for you.' In alarm I decided to follow his advice. I went straight to Mr. Argento and told him of my plight. He prayed for me, and that day the craving for opium and drink left me. I became literally a new man in Christ. And I've been living for Him now for eighteen years."

On the Sunday morning that the meetings began, it was found that the new church was not large enough to hold the crowd. Many hung around the doors and windows all through the service. It was evident from the very first meeting that the Holy Spirit had come in unusual power. Sometimes there would be hundreds of people weeping at the same time. As I remember, the sin confessed appeared to be mainly along the line of neglected duty in prayer and Bible study and care for souls.

I came in contact with two demon-possessed people during the Kwangchow meetings. One was the wife of a prominent evangelist. The evangelist was asked one day to take charge of the early morning prayer-meeting. Just after he had got the meeting nicely started his wife cried out: "You're a pretty one to be leading a prayer-meeting after the way you've sinned." She then proceeded to rake up all his past sins, including those which he had committed before his conversion, and, in fact, before he had even met her. "Yes," replied the evangelist, addressing the evil spirit, "while I was your slave I did these things. But I am your slave no longer. The Lord Jesus has changed my heart."

On another occasion, right in the middle of a meeting, this woman began to shout all manner of blasphemous things and generally to make a great ado. A Bible-woman, who was sitting behind her, pulled her down and told her to stop. With that she turned around and spat all over the Bible-woman. A lady-missionary, sitting near-by, took out her handkerchief and wiped the saliva off the Bible-woman's clothes. This so affected the demon-possessed that she put her head on the missionary's shoulder and wept bitterly.

The other demon-possessed person was a heathen, who had been brought into the meetings by his Christian friends in the hope that he might be cured. While nothing out of the ordinary was going on in a meeting this man was silent, save for a slight whimpering. But whenever the Spirit of God began to move in convicting power and people started to weep and confess their sins, he was roused into a great fury. The filth that then proceeded from his lips was frightful. After one meeting, in which he had been more than usually disturbing, the demon-possessed man was led into a room, where another missionary and myself together with most of the Chinese leaders had gathered.

Mr. M——— led in prayer. For some time the demon-possessed man merely went on whimpering. Then the missionary happened to use the expression, "Jesus of Nazareth," and immediately the man seemed to fall into the most excruciating agony. The same was true when Elder Wen prayed for him. Whenever the words "Jesus of Nazareth" were used he seemed to pass beyond all control. Finally, Elder Chang, putting his hand on the man's head, cried: "Foul fiend, in the name of Jesus Christ of Nazareth, come out of him." With that, the man flung himself on the floor and wallowed there, foaming at the mouth. There was a circle around him, and on account of the long Chinese clothes I could not see him closely; but suddenly I distinctly heard a sound as if he had vomited. Later on I looked carefully but there was no evidence that he had done so. Yet something, apparently, had gone out of him. He got up from the floor, assisted by several of the evangelists. He was limp, pale and trembling—but he was in his right mind. There was no doubt about that. The evangelist's wife was also prayed for in the same way, and the demon cast out of her. The report, a year later, was that both of these people were living as ordinary Christians.

During the eight days that the meetings lasted, 154 people were baptised; and some hundreds had already been baptised that year. One day some prominent business men from the city, who had been attending the church for years but had not had sufficient courage to take a definite stand, came to the missionary and asked that the rules of the church, which provided that a man should have made public confession for at least six months before being allowed to receive baptism, should be set aside in their case. "We've been a little uncertain about the Gospel up till now," they said, "but these days all our doubts have been removed. We truly believe that we have been baptised with the Holy Ghost; and we can't bear to have to wait six months before being received into the Church. Won't you receive us now?" They were accepted and baptised. Four years later, the two thousand Christians had increased to eight thousand.

During the meetings my attention was repeatedly drawn to a splendid looking specimen of manhood, a Mr. Yang. I inquired about him and learned that he had been a prize-fighter in his unconverted days. It had been his proud and undisputed boast that no man in all the surrounding counties could knock him out. He had naturally had many enemies; who, however, had taken good care to keep out of his way. Then he became a Christian, and his enemies decided that the time had come to wipe out old scores. One day, while Yang was at market, a group of them surrounded him, beat him almost to death and left him. He was found by some of his friends and carried back to his home. The missionaries wished to have the perpetrators of the outrage arrested and brought before the magistrate, but Mr. Yang refused to bring any charge against them. What he did was to pray for them.

In a few months he was well enough to go around again. His enemies were furious. They thought that had done for him. This time they decided that they would go right to his home and finish him off. The poor fellow was so terribly beaten up this second time that for months his family despaired of his life. Yet he was firmly insistent that no action should be taken against his assailants. As soon as he had recovered, he went around the country preaching the Gospel. He died a few years after I met him. But it was not before he had led many of his old enemies to Christ. He left a Church of six hundred members in his own village, and ten other churches scattered throughout the surrounding country.

I was asked to lead a series of meetings at Sinyangchou, extending over twelve days. In a few days the Holy Spirit seemed to be deeply convicting the schoolgirls and adult church members. On the sixth day an unusually intense movement took place among the girls. From their confessions it seemed as if they felt that they were indeed before the judge.

The schoolboys, however, remained as cold as stone. There were about a hundred of them in the High School, the majority of whom were from heathen families. They keenly resented, I was informed, my talking about their own peculiar sins and shortcomings, as if there were no others to be mentioned. As a matter of fact, I had really no idea what their sins were. I just spoke, day by day, along whatever line I felt prompted by the Holy Spirit, without referring to any one sin in particular. Still, whatever I said seemed to rub the boys the wrong way; and as the days went by it became evident that they had determined, as far as possible, not to listen to me.

As soon as I would start to speak they would look at each other with the most bored expressions on their faces, or close their eyes as if in sleep, or gaze up at the ceiling as if to say, "Well, no matter what he says, he can't make us listen to him." It usually happened, though, that presently a boy here and there would come under conviction, much to the annoyance, needless to say, of the more hardened. After every service the boys would return to their dormitory and hold an indignation meeting. "The impudence!" they would say, "of this man to come here and publish our sins abroad." Some, I learned, expressed a most intense desire to knife me. Each of these conclaves, of course, ended with a unanimous decision not to listen to me, and with the passing of resolutions inflicting all maner of penalties upon any who should yield.

I was sorry for the boys. I knew it was simply a contest between the Lord and the devil. And though I was hearing about the indignation meetings I thought it best not to make any reference to them. I had confidence in the power of Holy Spirit to make these boys yield, no matter how firmly they had resolved to oppose Him. One thing that gave me hope was that each succeeding day a larger number of the boys seemed to become uneasy. This naturally maddened the boys who were as yet unmoved, and after each service these would do their utmost to bring the wavering ones back to their senses.

The break came suddenly and unexpectedly. On the tenth afternoon, after the boys had gone back to their dormitory, the Holy Spirit came down amongst them with resistless power. Teachers and pupils alike were broken as by judgment. Boys in agony would plead with their teachers to pray for them. Teachers, weeping, would reply, "We're too full of sin ourselves to open our mouths before God." Fortunately, my evangelist, Mr. Su, was living right in the same dormitory, and knew just how to handle such a situation. He went from boy to boy doing what he could to help and comfort. The movement lasted for six hours. Mr. Su told me afterwards that he had never witnessed such a mighty manifestation of the controlling power of God over men.

It was a pretty subdued lot of boys that I came before on the eleventh forenoon. After I had finished my address, the boys vied with each other in their eagerness to give their testimonies. One after another confessed, in tears, how I had so cut them to the quick that they had wished they could only get close enough to me to stab me to death. For well over an hour the stream of testimony and confession continued. Truly had the Lord triumphed gloriously. During those last few days the students clung to me as to a father. They repeatedly declared their willingness to give their lives for Mr. Su or myself.

Chapter IX

HINDRANCES SWEPT AWAY WHEN THE SPIRIT WORKED IN CHIHLI

At a special gathering for prayer, which was held prior to the beginning of the main series of meetings at Pao-tingfu, the missionaries of this station were so deeply moved that I was convinced that there could be no sin on their part which would be likely to hinder the Lord's work there. Among other confessions there was one from Dr. L————. The doctor told us how that one afternoon he had gone to the street chapel in the city on his daily visit. On this particular occasion he had been detained at the compound and was an hour late. But he took it for granted that the evangelist would have gone ahead and opened the doors and be preaching to the people. He arrived to find the doors closed and the evangelist sleeping in one of the rear rooms.

"Naturally," said Dr. L————, "I was not a little annoyed; and I must admit I spoke with considerable heat. 'Is it possible,' I said to him, 'that just because I don't turn up you have no desire to save your people and that you are willing to let them perish in their sins?'" At that, it seems, the evangelist became deeply offended. "Reckon accounts!" he cried. "I'm not going to stay here any longer under a foreigner if he treats me like this." "Well, when I saw how he took it," Dr. L———— went on, "I humbled myself to the dust and begged him to stay. He has stayed on, but he has been in the huffs ever since and of absolutely no use so far as the work is concerned."

Listening to Dr. L————'s confession, I thought to myself that, having humbled himself before the evangelist, there was nothing else that he could be expected to do to make matters straight. Still, as the meetings progressed, I became conscious of a very serious hold-up among the people. I had just come from the mighty movement at

Changtehfu, Honan, and the deep spirituality of the Paotingfu missionaries had led me to expect the same results here. But day by day went by and, although there was evidence of stirrings here and there, still I knew that the full, mighty sweep of the Spirit's power had been denied us.

We came to the final meeting. I had given my address, and the meeting was open for prayer. In the conduct of these meetings I experience, as a rule, no overburdening anxiety. I tell myself that if God does not choose to use this or that address to move His people, then He will probably use the one to follow. And if in some particular meeting no spiritual power becomes evident in the prayers then I close that meeting and wait upon God for an outpouring of His grace in the next one. This evening, however, there was a great burden upon me, and I found myself agonising with God that He would remove the stone of hindrance, whatever it might be.

Dr. L—— was leaning on the pulpit beside me. "Doctor!" I whispered, "I simply cannot account for the hindrance in your church. I've always had a conviction, in leading these meetings, that once all the foreign missionaries have removed any hindering things from their midst, then no power of the devil can prevent the Holy Spirit from being made manifest. Certainly, listening to you missionaries at your prayer-meetings, I cannot imagine how there could be any hindrance on your part. Still, there is something holding us up."

"Why, it seems to me," replied Dr. L—— "that from what we have seen these days, we have reason to praise God for all eternity. You remember, on that second morning, how all those students fell around me in heaps, so mightily were they convicted. And then, on the fourth night, don't you remember how those hundred schoolgirls were so greatly moved? Besides, right from the beginning, there seems to have been just one stream of confession. Surely, then, we have the best of reasons to be grateful to God." "All the same," I insisted, "I feel somehow that you people have not received God's fulness yet."

I continued to pray, almost feverishly, that God would take the hindering stone away. Then suddenly a voice seemed to rebuke me. "Why all this anxiety? What are you fretting yourself about? Am I not sovereign? Can I not do My own work? Don't you know enough to 'stand still and see the salvation of the Lord?'" "Yes, Lord," I replied, "I'll do as you say. I'm tired out. I'll not even pray. I'll just 'stand still.'"

Presently a lady missionary, whose bursts of bad temper were notorious throughout the mission, rose and in great brokenness prayed that God would remove the hindering thing from her life. Right after her another lady missionary confessed to her lack of love for the people to whom she had come to minister, and pleaded that to her, too, grace might be given and the obstacle taken away. Then Miss L——, the Chinese head-teacher of the Girls' School, whom all thought to be about as perfect a Christian as it was possible to find, confessed in tears to her selfishness and the unworthiness of the example which she was setting to her girls.

By this time Dr. L—— was completely broken up. "O heavenly Father," he cried now, "forgive Thy sinning servant. I have spoken unadvisedly with my lips and hurt a Chinese brother. Thou knowest, O God, how that a long time ago Thy servant Moses spoke unadvisedly with his lips, and Thou didst punish him by not permitting him to enter the Promised Land. But only Moses was punished; the people did not suffer for his sin. The people were permitted to enter the land of blessing. Now, therefore, O God, punish Thy servant before Thee in like manner; but let not Thy people be hindered from obtaining the promised blessing."

Scarcely had the doctor ended when a man fell to the floor of the church with a terrible cry. It was the huffy evangelist. The next moment a man in another part of the audience was affected in precisely the same way. This time it was the Chinese principal of the Boys' School, one who had been undermining Dr. L——'s authority and endeavouring to work up rebellion among the students. In a few minutes men and women all over the building were falling on their knees and confessing their sins. One of the older boys cried, "Get down on your knees," and they all went down. On my left were the girls. Suddenly, without a word of command, like a wind sweeping over a field of grain, they, too, fell on their knees. Soon it seemed to me as if every last man, woman and child was down on the floor of that church crying for mercy.

That afternoon Dr. L—— had finished his work at the hospital and was setting out for the church when his attention was arrested by a strange sound. At first he thought it must be the noise of an express train coming in from the North. On going a little farther he decided that he had been mistaken and supposed that it was a tornado sweeping down upon the city. He arrived at the church and there he discovered that the strange sound was the sound of a people pleading with God.

The question might very well be asked—why was it necessary, apparently, that Dr. L—— should have made that public confession that evening? This was something that puzzled me at the time, and it was not till months later that I was afforded the explanation. Dr. L——, besides being a giant in intellect and a master of the Chinese language, was renowned far and wide for his Christian piety. And it seems that, after that apparently trifling set-to which he had had with his evangelist, it had become bandied about among the Chinese that "even such a man as Dr. L—— had a little of the old Adam temper in him." God's gifts were, therefore, withheld until a public confession from His servant had cleared the disgrace to His name.

The native pastor at Paotingfu (south suburb), and one of the foreign missionaries had invited me to their church to hold a series of revival meetings. I had accepted the invitation, not knowing at the time that the senior missionary was opposed to any such meetings. On the evening before the meetings were to begin I called upon this missionary in order to arrange for a daily prayer-meeting for the foreign leaders. "Before we agree to have a prayer-meeting," he said, "I want to have a clear understanding. I don't like to be the fellow prayed at. Our methods of approach are totally different. You work on the emotions. I go after the intellect. But I'll go in with you to these meetings if you agree to my proposition. It is that you should drop all your prepared addresses, and that we four pastors, yourself included, of course, should have public discussions every day instead. We'll decide on a subject— say 'The Kingdom of God.' Let one talk on, e.g., what is the meaning of the Kingdom of God. Another might give an address on how we can bring the Kingdom of God to pass. Then, after we leaders have expressed our views, we will have some singing and perhaps a little prayer, and then dismiss the meeting. If you will agree to that—just to meet me for a general discussion each day—then I will go in with you. But otherwise—no!"

"But you have known for months," I replied, "that I had been invited here and that I had promised to come. During all this time I have received no objection from you to my method of conducting meetings. Surely then, on the very eve of this series, it would be almost unreasonable to expect me to drop all the addresses that I had prepared for your people."

"I fully expected you to turn down my proposition," said the missionary, "and therefore I'll have nothing to do with the meetings." I was quite at a loss to account for his attitude. Within sight of the church were the graves of seventeen foreign and Chinese leaders who had suffered martyrdom in 1900. Yet, judging by the pitiable condition to which the church had fallen, they seemed to have died in vain. One Sunday morning, not long before my arrival, there had been a free fight among the Chinese leaders after the morning service. One of the deacons had been seriously injured. And yet this brother did not seem to care. He wanted to "get after the intellect." "But surely,"

I said, as I was leaving, "we are to have a prayer-meeting?"
"No!" he replied most emphatically, "we are not."

For the first day or two it was quite evident that the
Holy Spirit was being grieved and hindered. For one
thing, the students gave a lot of trouble. There were about
fifty of them. Knowing that the senior missionary was
opposed to the meetings, they had decided to do as they
pleased. It was impossible to keep any order among them.
It just seemed as if the devil had taken hold of them. Late
in the evening of the fourth day I was in my room preparing an address on the subject, "Quench not the Spirit,"
when a message was brought to me. It was from the missionary who had arranged for the meetings. All it said
was, "Come quickly to the Boys' School. I'm in trouble."

As I was hurrying over to the school I wondered to myself what could be the matter. I knew that this missionary had charge of the prayer-meeting in the school that
evening, but he struck me as being the last man in the
world who was calculated to set an audience on fire. What,
then, could have happened?

On entering the school, a strange spectacle met my eyes.
The boys were all, without exception, crying at the top of
their voices and pounding the desks before them with both
hands. The missionary was looking on, quite helpless. I
asked him how this had come about, and he replied: "I
was just quietly leading the prayer-meeting when suddenly
one boy after another broke out weeping. I tried to get
them to sing, but they wouldn't sing. Finally, in despair, I
sent for you." I said I wasn't quite sure what to do myself. For a while I just waited and prayed that God would
reveal His will in the matter.

Presently one of the boys would stop pounding his desk,
go over to another boy and say, "Please forgive me for
that row we had yesterday. It was all my fault." Then
one would take a pencil out of his desk, go over to another
and say, "This is your pencil. I stole it." Another would
go over to his school-mates and say, "I've been speaking a
lot of nasty things about you behind your back. Please
forgive me."

This went on for over half an hour. When I saw that it was about over I felt that it was time for me to interfere. The teachers had gathered by this time, so we started up some choruses. But the boys paid no heed. They did not even seem to hear us. Then I took the big school-bell and rang it with all my might. Still they paid no heed. Right in the centre of the room there was a rickety table piled high with slates. I went over to the table and shook it as if I were going to knock everything to pieces. That caused some of them to look up. I caught their eyes and said, "Boys, stop crying!" They obeyed, and in this way the movement gradually subsided. We then sang a hymn and I said, "Now, boys, you had better get off to bed."

For the rest of the meetings those boys behaved like angels. On the morning following this incident, I gave an address on "Quench not the Holy Spirit." The whole audience seemed to be deeply moved. One after another, the quarrelsome leaders got up before the church, and in tears confessed their faults one to another. The rule in that mission was that candidates for baptism must be on probation for at least six months; but so manifest to all had been the work of the Holy Spirit in the hearts of the students that the regulation was temporarily set aside, and on the Sunday after my departure forty-four of them were baptized.

The missionaries at Hwailu had been through the Boxer year, having had the most remarkable deliverances. I had every confidence that the Lord was going to move mightily at Hwailu. Yet it soon became evident that here, too, there was a very serious hindrance somewhere. I was informed that there were grave quarrels within the bounds of the mission, prominent leaders being among the chief offenders. As the meetings progressed these leaders, realising how they were holding things up, got together and tried to make matters right. One of their number, however, was as stubborn as a man could be. He would listen to nothing and would give way in nothing.

On the fifth day, in the middle of a meeting, this man suddenly gave vent to strange sounds, and made as if to bore his head into the ground. At once I turned to Mr. Green and asked him if the man was accustomed to have epileptic fits. "No," he replied. "Then have him taken out," I said. "The only thing it can be is demon possession." Mr. Green spoke to some helpers, who went and laid hold of the man in order to lead him out of the church. With that he became furious. He vowed he was going to kill Mr. Green and all his family. He would never rest, he cried, until he had wiped them out.

I asked the man who had taken charge of the poor fellow to pray for him in the hope that the demon might be cast out. It was only with the greatest difficulty that they managed to drag him out of the church to a room near-by. They told me afterwards that, as they prayed for the man, there would be times when he seemed to be filled with great terror. "Save me, save me!" he could cry. "I'm slipping into hell." Again fierce turns would come to him, and nothing would do but that he would exterminate the whole Green family. Often he would attempt to bore his head into the ground, as he had done in the church. At other times he would try to climb up the wall of the room feet first. Hour after hour through these various changes the Christians kept on praying. Finally the demon was cast out.

The following day, which was the last day of the meetings, this man was amazingly changed. He was now willing to go further than any of the other leaders. No mere patching up of the quarrels would do for him. He wished to see the matter settled right to its very foundations and everything cleared away so that the Holy Spirit could move unimpeded in their hearts.

When we sat down for supper that last evening we were not a very optimistic party. Certainly the results at Hwailu had not been nearly what I had hoped for or expected. At each meal we had been in the habit of singing the chorus, "The Lion of Judah shall break every chain and give us the victory again and again." A visiting missionary tried to cheer us up. "Come on, Mrs. Green," he said, "let's have the old chorus once again." With that, Mrs. Green burst out weeping. "I can't sing it," she sobbed, "I'm too disappointed. I believed that, when Mr. Goforth came here to lead these meetings, all our hindrances would be swept away just as they were at Changteh and Paotingfu. But here it is all over now and our quarrels remain unsettled, and everything seems to be just the same as ever." The visiting missionary insisted, however, and the chorus was sung—Mrs. Green, in spite of her tears, joining in with us.

As we were rising from the table, Miss Gregg, one of the single ladies at Hwailu, entered the room. "I'm going to wind up my affairs here as soon as I can," she told us, "and I'm going right back to England. When I heard that Mr. Goforth was coming here to conduct revival meetings I told my Chinese sisters that the Lord would be sure to sweep away all our hindrances and give us abundant blessing. But here the meetings are all over and the quarrels remain unsettled. I'm so disappointed. I simply cannot face those women again. They trusted me so implicitly. So the only thing I can do is to go back to England."

Miss Gregg went on to tell us that about a year before a printed motto had been given her. She repeated it to us. As I remember, it ran something like this: "Whatever my Father sends me, be it joy or disappointment, no matter how hard it may be to bear, since I know it comes from my Father, I'm going to receive it with both hands joyfully." "During the course of this year," continued Miss Gregg, "the motto has become somewhat blurred. Well, this afternoon Miss ——, having a headache which prevented her from attending the service, repainted the motto in the most beautiful ornamental letters and hung it on the wall opposite the door of my room so that I would be certain to see it as soon as I entered. Well, when I opened the door and saw that motto hanging there—it was just too much. I went right over and turned its face to the wall. I simply couldn't bring myself to receive such a disappointment as this 'with both hands joyfully.' "

"Miss Gregg," I said, "I think I am beginning to see where the hindrance lies. You had heard how God had moved at Changteh and Paotingfu and elsewhere, and you made up your mind that He must do a similar work here in Hwailu or so disappoint you that you would throw up your work and go back to England. In other words, as far as you were concerned, God had no option. He must please you in your own way or else lose your service. Remember that God is sovereign. He can never lay aside His sovereign will and authority. I understand that Mr. Green is out there now in the tent holding a prayer-meeting with the Christians. How do you know but that at this very moment every hindrance has been removed?"

Just as I finished speaking Mr. Green came bounding into the room crying, "Hallelujah!" "All quarrels have been made up," he said, "and every hindering thing laid away; and they're all waiting out there in the tent for you people to come and rejoice with them over what God has done." Miss Gregg didn't wait for him to finish. She was already on her way to the tent. Since then Miss Gregg has been mightily used all over China in this movement for the deepening of the spiritual life.

For various reasons I think it would be better for me to leave unmentioned the name of the next station visited. Few more painful or more depressing experiences have fallen to my lot in China than during the meetings which I conducted there. The missionaries had become notorious through their quarrelling. And, as if that were not pitiful enough, the Chinese Christians had taken sides.

On the first day of the meetings an evangelist, who had been through the Changtehfu revival and had been deeply moved then, made an earnest plea to the congregation. "Brethren," he cried, "by our quarrels and divisions we are quenching the Holy Spirit and letting God's work here go to pieces. I tell you I am willing to do anything to make peace. I am willing to get down and kow-tow to any one who has anything against me. But, brethren, do let us give way to the Spirit of God and remove all these hindering things from our midst." Never have I listened to anything more moving. It seemed that all concerned in the quarrels must surely yield and get right with one another. But no one paid the slightest heed.

Again, on the fourth day, the evangelist, in a veritable agony of weeping, pleaded with his fellow-Christians to forgive one another and allow the love of God to be shed abroad in their hearts. This time the women in the audience seemed to be somewhat moved, but the men remained as cold as ice. When I left that place it was with the sad conviction that the devil remained in full control.

While I was at this last place the senior missionary happened to be on furlough. It seems that shortly before his return the junior missionary, with whom he was at enmity, moved out so as to be away before the other's arrival. As the junior missionary was on his way to the station the Chinese who stood in with the senior missionary followed the young men, jeering at him and pelting him with clods. When the senior missionary returned a few days later the Chinese on the other side pelted him with manure and any kind of filth which they could lay their hands on. Not long after, this missionary had the greatest difficulty in keeping his "Christians" from taking sword and spear in hand and killing each other. No missionary lives there now.

CHAPTER X

FURTHER EVIDENCES OF THE SPIRIT'S MIGHTY WORK IN CHIHLI

FOR the first few days at Siaochang I was caused considerable annoyance by a certain prominent man in the congregation who had a habit of praying at every n.eeting as soon as I finished my address. The prayer was always the same; I could discern no prompting of the Holy Spirit in it. I tried to silence the man by issuing a warning at each meeting against any person praying unless definitely directed to do so by the Holy Spirit. I pointed out that it was God's will to glorify His Son through every one getting utterance, and that if a small group took it upon themselves to do all the praying many would necessarily be deprived of the privilege. In spite of such broad hints, this man was always the first to lead off in prayer.

On the sixth day it was quite evident, from the strained, anxious look on many faces as I was speaking, that the Holy Spirit was working powerfully in the people's hearts. I felt that the time of real blessing was at hand. Yet, as soon as the meeting was opened for prayer, this man jumped to his feet and began to pray. He gave utterance to a few ordinary platitudes, and seemed so evidently under Satan's influence that I felt called upon to stop him. "Please sit down, sir," I said, "and give those who are moved by the Holy Spirit a chance to pray." He stopped on the instant and resumed his seat. Whereupon dozens all over the audience broke out into prayer and confession.

After the meeting the man came to me, very humble and penitent. "I can only thank God that you stopped me," he said, "because truly the devil had got into me. I have been backsliding badly of late. I have been taking opium. I am a thief . . . During these meetings I have become more and more anxious. I felt that I simply had to confess my sins; and yet I knew very well that if I did so my reputation would be lost. So at each meeting the devil would come to my rescue and say, 'Pray.' I would obey, and immediately all sense of conviction would pass away. Today, during your address, I was in an awful state. My sins appeared appalling, and I felt that this time nothing could prevent me from blurting them out. But when you finished speaking the devil almost pushed me forward to pray. I hardly knew what I was saying. Then I heard you tell me to sit down. I knew then that the game was up, and that there was no use holding out any longer. I've told you the story, and tomorrow I want to repeat it before the whole congregation."

On the following morning he rose as usual at the conclusion of my address, but this time there was no question about the nature of the Spirit that was guiding him. His confession, needless to say, made a deep impression upon the people. In fact, the matron of the Girls' School was so broken and in such agony over her sins that it was feared for a time that she would lose her mind. Confession, however, brought relief. She told us that while she was at school in Peking, in 1900, the Boxers wiped out her whole family. She had an idea who the murderers were, and for years had been constantly planning how to take revenge. Now, however, she declared, the Spirit of Love had touched her heart, and she would gladly forgive them.

There was a strong group of evangelists in the church at Siaochang. Day after day these evangelists would get up, apparently under deep feeling, and giving the impression that they were about to bring something terrible to light. Instead, their prayers would be invariably of the tamest variety. They would run something like this: "O Lord, I'm a great sinner. Thou knowest how I have hindered Thy cause. Have mercy on me. Amen." Nothing specific ever came to the surface.

On the seventh evening two of the evangelists came to interview me, having been sent as a deputation by their colleagues. "We evangelists," they said, "have been confessing our sins these days, and somehow we do not seem to get any peace out of it. We have come to ask your opinion about it, and to see if you can help us." "I want to ask you one question," I replied; "have you committed these sins, you speak of, by the bundle or have you deliberately grieved the Holy Spirit and committed them one by one?" "Why, of course," they said, "we've committed them one by one and not by the bundle." "Very well, brethren," I said, "since you are leaders in the church, I believe it is the Spirit's will that you should confess your sins, as you have committed them, one by one."

"But that would never do!" they cried in dismay. "Why, there's murder, there's robbery, there's adultery— to be confessed. It would wreck the church if we were to do as you say." "I'm sorry," I said, "but I can take no responsibility for that. I'm simply telling you what I believe to be the will of God in present circumstances."

They went away. Next day the evangelists continued to pray in the same vague fashion. The price of victory was too great to pay. Two years later, owing to a deficit in the home treasury, the usual grant failed to come, and ten of the evangelists were sent home to seek other employment.

The services at Peking (American Presbyterian) were hindered, as they had been at Siaochang, by a certain individual insisting upon leading off each time a meeting was thrown open for prayer. The offender in this instance was a prominent evangelist. At every meeting I would warn the people to beware lest it was the devil and not the Holy Spirit that was prompting them to pray. I would point out that in a large audience only a limited number could be heard; so that a man, after he had prayed once or twice, should be patient and give others a chance. But my warnings went unheeded. The evangelist was invariably the first on his feet. He seemed to realize that his was no ordinary eloquence. His prayers, indeed, were given with real oratorical effect. But it was quite evident that the Holy Spirit had nothing to do with them, and not till the end of time could any one be moved by them.

At last, in despair, I said to one of the missionaries, "Won't you speak to that evangelist quietly and ask him to be patient for a few meetings and give other people a chance to pray?" "What!" he cried. "You surely don't expect me to go and rebuke that man of all people? Why, he has the most frightful temper. It is so bad, in fact, that in his church not a single convert has been added since he took charge. No, I really wouldn't have the nerve to go and say anything to him. I'm afraid the only thing to do is just to leave him alone."

What might be termed the climax of the meetings was reached on the sixth day. None but the coldest and most unresponsive could help but feel aware of God's presence that day. Most moving of all, perhaps, was the heart-broken confession of an evangelist who for days had been under deep conviction. "During the Boxer year," he said, "I was out preaching in a certain district some distance from my home. In my absence a band of Boxers came and killed my mother and father and wife and children, and burnt my home. When I returned all that was left to me was ashes. I discovered who had led the band, and a friend of mine waylaid him at night and hacked him to bits. The man had two sons, and my friend was for killing them as well and making a clean sweep of it. But the neighbours managed to hide them from us.

"For his crime my friend was forced to flee outside the borders of China. Before he left, it was agreed that I should search for the children, and that as soon as I found them I would write to him and he would come back secretly and do away with them. We would then be able to say that our revenge was complete. Two years passed before I finally located the hiding-place of the boys. As soon as I knew definitely where to lay hold of them I went to Dr. Sheffield and told him about it. I supposed that he would suggest that we should hand them right over to the official and have them executed. But, to my utter amazement, he said, 'Good! I am glad that you have found them. You will now be able to care for them and send them to school.' I could scarcely believe my ears. What could be more horrible, I thought, than that I should be the means of educating the children of the man who killed my mother and father and my wife and my children? I left Dr. Sheffield in a towering rage.

"The next day a letter came from my friend who was living in Siberia. 'Here I have to remain in exile all my life,' he wrote, 'because I undertook to avenge your wrongs. You agreed with me that you would find those two boys and have me come back secretly and kill them. But two years have gone by, and you haven't found them yet. You haven't done your part. There's no filial piety about you. I refuse to consider you as my friend any longer.'

"On receiving this letter," went on the evangelist, "I resolved that I would have my friend come back and murder the two boys. But since then the very root of prayer has been taken out of my life. During these meetings I have become more and more troubled and anxious. God has shown me plainly that if I won't forgive my enemies, then He can't forgive me. I'm in an awful state. I can't eat or sleep. Won't some of you people pray for me?"

It was a most moving confession. When he finished, there were people sobbing here and there, all over the audience. I found my own voice breaking when I said, "Now will some one who is truly led of the Spirit of God pray for this brother?" Immediately up jumped the eloquent evangelist. For a minute or two I allowed him to go on; hoping against hope that the Spirit of God had moved him at last. But no, it was the same old oratorical prayer. "Brother!" I cried, "sit down! and give somebody who is moved by the Holy Spirit a chance to pray." He took his seat, and there followed many intense, heartfelt prayers for the one in distress.

At the close of the meeting I was told that there was a
gentleman in one of the rooms who wished to speak to
me. On being led to the room I found the eloquent
evangelist awaiting me. He was literally boiling over
with rage. Shaking his fist in my face, he cried, "I've
found you out at last, Pastor Goforth. You were led by
the devil in your meetings in Manchuria, and you're being
led by the devil here, too." Without saying a word in
reply I turned and left him. The last I heard of him he
was begging on the streets of Peking.

While passing through Peking, on my way back from
the Manchurian Revival, I was asked by the American
Board people to give an account of the movement one
Sunday morning in their church. During the open session
that followed my address one of the High School girls
made a most remarkable prayer. In substance it was
something like this: "O Lord, we praise Thee for pouring
out Thy Spirit upon Manchuria. The ground was dry and
parched outside the wall, and there was crying need for
blessing. But we, inside the wall,[1] are just as dry and
parched. May the showers of blessing fall upon us too.
We plead with Thee—do not pass us by." As the girl
was praying she was not weeping, but it was easy to see
that she was very near the breaking-point. Her voice and
manner were such that I could not refrain from watching
her. There was something about her face that won and
at the same time humbled one. An unusual light shone
there. One of the missionaries whispered to me at the
close of the service, ". . . her face was like that of an
angel." Her principal told me that the girl showed very
ordinary talent in her studies, but that among her school-
mates she truly walked in the footsteps of the Master.

Some months later, at the invitation of the missionaries,
I returned to the same church to conduct a week of special
meetings. Right at the start I became aware of a very
serious hindrance. The Chinese pastor gave me a hint
as to its nature, but it was not until the meetings were

[1] The reference is to the Great Wall of China.

over that I became acquainted with all the details. It
seemed that the deacons, as a body, were opposed to the
meetings. They did not believe in public confessions,
they said. Such things could only be prompted by the
devil. They were going to keep away from the meetings,
they declared, and persuade all their friends to do like-
wise.

It happened that the deacons had a very good reason
for avoiding public confession. When the foreign armies
had captured Peking, in 1900, the Empress Dowager and
the Emperor and all the great ones of the Manchu dynasty
had fled precipitately to a western province, leaving the
royal palace with all its priceless valuables unguarded.
Among those who had availed themselves of this golden
opportunity for personal enrichment had been certain
deacons of the American Board Church. At the time of
my meetings the Empress Dowager was back in Peking;
and well those deacons knew that, in a public meeting,
under pressure from the Holy Spirit, there was small like-
lihood of their sin remaining covered up. Yes, they certainly had a potent reason for avoiding anything like a
Holy Ghost revival.

As the meetings progressed some measure of spiritual
activity became discernible, but there was lacking that
unexplainable something which is always realised when
the Holy Spirit has swept away all hindrances. We came
to the last service. I had given my address and the meeting was open for prayer. Suddenly the schoolgirl, who
had made that remarkable prayer months before, began
to pray. Her heart seemed agonised. It was scarcely possible to catch her words through her sobs. "O Father in
Heaven," she cried, "here we have come to the end of
these meetings and still the hindrance remains. It seems
that Jesus our Savior is not to be glorified as He ought.
Our leaders will not humble themselves and get right with
Thee. So the blessing has been withheld from us. O Father, is it a sacrifice that You are waiting for? If it is,
then let me be the victim. I am willing that You should

blot my name right out of the Book of Life, if through my sacrifice the hearts of the people might be opened to Thee."

As the girl was praying, cries could be heard from all over the audience. I knew that some of the deacons were there that evening. How could they possibly resist that dear girl's plea? I thought. But not one of them stirred, and I closed the meeting.

During the meetings at Peking (Methodist Episcopal) my audiences were made up largely of students from the university, which was connected with the mission. The students, I was led to understand, really considered themselves above such things as revival meetings; but attended out of curiosity. "Up till now," they told one another, "this missionary has only come in contact with boys and girls who had no minds of their own. It might have been easy enough for him to manipulate them and cause them to disgrace themselves by confessing their sins. But he is up against a different proposition with us university students. We will show him that his hypnotism will not work on every one."

As the meetings progressed, the rank and file of the Christians gave evidence, at times, of a desire to get rid of hindering things. But the university students remained throughout quite unmoved. Certainly, when the meetings came to an end, none of us could honestly say that the results were exceeding abundant beyond all that we had asked or thought. I had to leave for England immediately after the closing service. Before going, I urged Dr. Pike, a man who in former years had been mightily used of God in revival work, to continue the meetings until the hindrance had been removed. I pointed out that to stop then would be to make our effort appear largely as a triumph for the devil. Dr. Pike laid the matter before the other missionaries, and it was decided to go on with the meetings.

On the twelfth day the preachers and evangelists were all broken up and confessed their faults one to another. Then the Spirit of God, I am told, swept like an avalanche

through the university students. They confessed how
hardened their hearts had been, and that in all their
opposition they had been directed by the Evil One. The
movement among them was so intense, so general, that
for days it was found impossible to go on with the lectures. In this room and that impromptu prayer-meetings
would start up at five o'clock in the morning, and similar meetings would continue until ten o'clock at night.
When the holidays came, one hundred and fifty of these
students toured the surrounding country, two by two,
proclaiming the Gospel of the Grace of God. Another
year, I understand, a number of them had gone round the
country selling cigarettes.

Pengcheng is a noted pottery center in southwest Chihli;
its fame, it might be added, being derived not merely
from the products of its kilns but also from the notoriously wicked character with which the name of the city has
for centuries been associated. It was the northernmost
station of my old field in Central China. I visited the
city for the first time in 1890, but it was quite a few years
before the work there began to assume encouraging pro-
portions.

In 1915 I decided to hold a week of special meetings at
Pengcheng for the purpose of arousing the Christians.
On learning of my intention, some prominent business
men connected with the Board of Trade arranged that we
should have the use of the Board of Trade building, an
old disused temple. A large mat pavilion was erected, at
their expense, right in the temple yard. The temple—
unfortunately as I thought—was situated at some distance from the city, and I was afraid, when I learned of
the arrangements that had been made, that it would be
impossible to draw the crowd out that far.

Yet from the very first meeting the pavilion was
crammed. The Christians were most responsive. They
came under conviction, confessed their sins, acknowledged their faults one to another and made restitution
for wrongs done. This had a startling effect upon the

unsaved. Men and women by the score confessed their belief in Jesus Christ for the first time. Among these were several noted scholars and a number of prominent kiln owners. Over fifty names in all were taken down as catechumens, but many more were rejected as not being sufficiently instructed. Evangelist Ho, who had been with me ever since the opening of the work at Pengcheng, told me that while walking through the streets in the evening it seemed to him that every one was talking about "the strange happenings over in the temple yard." He thought that the people were all on the point of turning to God.

From Pengcheng I went direct to one[1] of the large centers of our mission, where I had been invited to conduct a ten days' series of meetings. It was a slack time of the year, and I expected, of course, that all the Christians from the neighbouring out-stations would be in for the meetings. Imagine my disappointment when I learned that little or no effort had been made to get them to attend. Throughout the meetings there were never more than ten Christians from the outside at any service.

At the missionary prayer-meeting, which I attended daily, little or no mention was made of the services which I was leading. The missionaries, one and all, seemed to be peculiarly indifferent to the need for a close touch with God in the life of their church. Even the missionary from whom I had received the invitation to lead the meetings showed plainly that he did not take the movement seriously. He seemed to be more concerned with the welfare of his dogs and pigeons than that God should pour out His Spirit in saving power upon His people.

At a certain meeting, while several in great brokenness were praying and confessing, I happened to notice this missionary staring in a surprised, almost amused, fashion at what was going on. My heart sank, for I knew that most certainly there would be trouble ahead. The Chinese are quick to notice anything like that, and, very

[1] This station is in Honan, not in Chihli. We insert it here to preserve the chronological sequence.

naturally, feel deep resentment. They conclude among
themselves that the meetings have been arranged special-
ly for their benefit, and that the foreigners consider they
have no sins to confess.

That evening, two of the evangelists came to see me.
Both were splendid men from the Changteh region. They
had been through the mighty movement at Changtsun
some years before. "We can't stay here any longer," they
said. "We are going back home. There's no use trying
to save souls here. There was that missionary today,
while our people were beginning to be broken up, staring
at us as if he thought the whole thing were a joke." I
pointed out to them that since the missionary did not
appear to be awake to the need for Divine blessing it was
all the more urgent that they, who had seen with their
own eyes what the Spirit of God was capable of doing,
should remain at their post. They promised me that they
would stay on.

The meetings came to an end, and, while not a few had
been blessed, there had clearly been nothing approaching
a sweeping spiritual movement. Some weeks later I
learned that the report had gone all around the mission
that "Mr. Goforth has lost his power. He preached for
ten days at ——, with hardly any result!" In this way
the missionaries of that station succeeded in clearing
themselves. But sometimes I wonder if it ever really
occurred to them that they might be in any way to blame.

The meetings at Shuntehfu followed immediately after
those referred to above. It was not long before I became
aware that there existed, here in Shuntehfu, an intense
desire on the part of missionaries and Chinese Christians
alike for God's richest blessing. The study of the missionary at whose house I stayed was situated directly below my room. Each morning, long before daylight, my
host's heart-earnest pleadings with God were borne up to
me. At a prayer-meeting this same missionary burst into
tears, saying, "Lord, I've come to the place where I would
rather pray than eat." And, with no exaggeration, that

seemed to be the prevailing spirit among all the missionaries. They appeared determined not to let God go until He had blessed them.

The same spirit, too, was characteristic of the Chinese Christians. At one of the early morning prayer-meetings the evangelist in charge said, "Brethren, you have been too eager to pray. You won't even wait until the one who is praying says 'Amen' before you start. You haven't given your sisters a chance. Again and again I've noticed some sister rising to pray only to have one of you men get in before her. Now this morning let it be clearly understood that the men will all pray quietly in their hearts and give the women a chance. The meeting is now open for our sisters to lead us in prayer." On the instant fully a dozen men started to pray, most of them in tears. It was impossible for one to draw any other conclusion than that the Spirit's pressure was so irresistible that they simply could not hold back.

During those days all manner of sin was confessed; wrongs were righted and quarrels made up. I saw old Confucian scholars, broken and humbled, come up on the platform and confess their Lord. Altogether five hundred men and women acknowledged Christ as Savior for the first time. It was, perhaps, the most remarkable movement of the Spirit which it has ever been my privilege to witness.

CHAPTER XI

GOD'S DEALINGS WITH YOUNG PEOPLE IN SHANTUNG

A MOVEMENT began at Putoupeichen and steadily increased in intensity until it finally reached a climax on the sixth day. I have been present at movements, e.g., at Shuntehfu, which have been more powerful, more far-reaching, perhaps, but none where I have felt so completely conscious of the Spirit's controlling power over a large body of people. It did seem that day as if every last vestige of opposition had been swept away and that Christ alone was exalted. We remained in this atmosphere for the remaining two days of the meetings.

A wonderful testimony meeting was held on the last evening. Spontaneous resolutions to new obedience were heard from many. One remarkable thing about these testimonies was the great number who claimed that, on that sixth morning when the Spirit's fire had swept so irresistibly through the audience, they had been healed of their bodily ailments. In my addresses I had made no special mention of Divine healing. Yet here was the testimony of these people that suddenly, at some crucial moment, that which ailed them passed away. On another occasion, in a neighbouring province, I heard similar testimonies to Divine healing. In both instances, according to the evidence of the witnesses, the experience coincided with the moment of most intense conviction.

The Chowtsun missionaries had been having considerable difficulty with their High School students. The boys had gone so far as to smash all the furniture in the school and burn the missionary headmaster in effigy. During my meetings the boys occupied the large choir loft behind me. They really sang unusually well. But while I was speaking I would notice traces of amusement on the faces of different ones in the audience. This led me to have a strong suspicion that the boys were cutting up. On questioning one of the missionaries, he replied that it was only too true.

On the third morning I had all the boys brought down and put in the seats right in front of me. They took this, quite naturally I suppose, as a great insult. When the singing began the whole school remained dumb. Not a boy opened his mouth. This continued all through the third day. The principal was very put out about it and asked me if he had not better command them to sing. "Not on any account," I replied. "The Spirit of God is going to make those boys yield and glorify their Master, and He will do it without either of us needing to lift a finger to help Him."

All through the fourth day the boys remained as dumb as posts. Judging from the cold, obstinate expression on their faces, it did seem as if they were a long way removed from the point of yielding. Yet, when I entered the church on the fifth morning it looked to me as if every last one of those boys was in tears. When I gave out the first hymn, oh, how spontaneously and lustily they sang! As soon as the meeting was opened for prayer, boy after boy came running up to the front to make confession of sin. Among other things they confessed to drinking, gambling and to visiting houses of ill fame. Some of the boys were so overcome that they had scarcely begun to pray when they fell to the floor in agony. After the meetings, the boys went in bands on Sundays and preached in the surrounding villages.

During the last four days of the meetings every prayer, every confession, every testimony seemed to be absolutely controlled by the Holy Spirit. One feature of the confessions that struck me forcibly was that so many of the Chinese leaders acknowledged the use of tobacco and whisky. In fact, it seemed to be almost general among them. At the dinner table, on the last day of the meetings, one of the lady missionaries put the question to me: "Do you really think it wrong to smoke?" "I don't quite see the necessity for asking me such a question," I replied. "Surely the Holy Spirit has made very plain these days what is the Lord's will in the matter. I might say, though, that in no place where I have been used hitherto have I listened to so many Chinese leaders confess to the use of tobacco and whisky as here in Chowtsun." "Well, but Spurgeon smoked!" she retorted, "and you couldn't get a better man than he was." "I'm sure none of us will deny that Spurgeon was a good man," I said, "but I'm equally sure that if he had only known at the time what a handle you people were going to make of his habit he would have got rid of it in short órder."

That ended the subject for the time being, but, just as I was leaving, a missionary, who had been present at the table when the above conversation took place, drew me aside and said, "I understand you are going to Chingchowfu. Now there are two missionaries at that station who are real saints of God. They both smoke, and I thought I would warn you that if you say anything about tobacco there it is bound to hurt them and it will only do more harm than good." "I'm sorry that I can't profit by your advice," I replied. "I will be giving an entirely different series of addresses at Chingchow from what I have given here. I cannot recall just now whether there is any mention of tobacco in them, but if there is, it will come out."

At Chingchowfu, as at Chowtsun, the schoolboys provided at first a strong element of opposition. There were usually five or six hundred students, male and female, present at the meetings, including a large number from the Normal School. On the very first day of the meetings the Spirit fell in convicting power upon a large number of the older church members. Day by day the movement increased in intensity, finally spreading among the schoolgirls. But the boys remained untouched. On the sixth day, when every one else in the building seemed to be broken, they sat looking on cold and unmoved. As I was giving my addresses I would constantly notice the

Normal School students, with their heads down, reading from books in their laps. I pleaded with them repeatedly to lay whatever they were reading aside and listen to what God had sent me there to say to them. For a little while they would pay attention and then down their heads would go again.

On the sixth evening, just as I was about to begin my address, one of the missionaries came up on the platform and asked for permission to say a few words. "I have again and again urged you people," he said, "to deny yourselves so that you might contribute more bountifully to the evangelistic fund and thus make it possible to bring the Gospel to the millions that are around us. But since these meetings began the Holy Spirit has been pointing out to me that while I smoke such expensive cigars I have no right to talk to you people about self-denial. I have resolved, therefore, to give up this useless luxury, and the money which hitherto I have spent on it will from now on go into the evangelistic fund." This was one of the missionaries concerning whom I had been warned not to say anything about tobacco lest I should hurt him. He was indeed a saint, but he gave no sign of being hurt that evening, and blessed indeed were all those who were privileged to listen to his words of self-denial.

On the seventh day one of the Normal School students came up on the platform carrying a pile of books. He flung them down with evident loathing, then, turning to the congregation, he cried, "These are 'devil' books. Some of us boys picked them up in the city. They are written for the express purpose of polluting the mind with vile thoughts. Through them I have been led to commit adultery. While these meetings have been going on the devil has prompted us boys to keep reading these books so that we wouldn't hear God's truth and be convicted of our sin." A definite breach had now been made in the opposition of the students. One after another came forward and in great brokenness told how they had been led astray by this vile literature. Hour after hour scores kept pressing toward the platform. Finally, after the meeting had lasted for five and a half hours, with dozens still waiting for an opportunity to confess, the missionaries practically compelled me to go away and take a rest.

On the forenoon of the eighth day, the stream of confession was such that I was not able to give an address. That evening the other missionary at the station came up to the platform and confessed that he, too, had come to see, during those days, how absurd it was for him to press upon his people the necessity for sacrifice when he was spending so much money upon tobacco. He declared that, like his brother missionary, we was going to give up the habit, and that henceforth the moncy which had been spent upon it was to be devoted to the evangelistic fund.

The evening before I left Chingchow I had supper at the home of this missionary. In the course of the meal he said to me: "My table-boy here has never professed faith in Christ, and during these meetings he has shown no signs of being deeply moved. I wonder if you would mind speaking to him?" "Very well," I said, "when he comes in to clear away the dishes you and the rest of the family go into the sitting-room, and I'll remain here and talk to him." "How is it," I began, by asking the boy when we were alone, "that you have not yielded to your Lord, when so many others have done so?" "But I have yielded," he replied, with a smile. "I was standing there among many others on that seventh evening until half-past twelve, waiting for a chance to confess; but then you stopped the meeting. What troubled me was that after I had decided to follow Christ I felt that I had nothing to give to Him. It didn't seem right that one who had died for me should receive nothing from me in return. But I didn't see how I could spare any money to give to Him; for I only get a few dollars a month, and I've got a wife and two children to keep. Then my master got up and told how he had determined to give up tobacco, and immediately I thought to myself, 'Why, of course I'll give up smoking, too, and just hand the extra money over to the Lord.' And since then I've been so happy that I've scarcely been able to contain myself for joy."

When I returned to the sitting-room and told the people there of the result of the interview, my host burst into tears. "I would give up a good deal more than tobacco," he said, "if I could bless others like that."

Unknown to the foreign missionaries or myself the Chinese leaders at Chefoo had agreed beforehand to discountenance all public confession in my meetings. They had concluded, they said, that such emotional movements, as had been the rule in Manchuria and Korea, could only be from the devil and not from the Holy Spirit. All the Christians were strictly warned not on any account to confess their sins publicly. When, on the fourth morning, several of the women began to show very evident signs of conviction, two of the deacons went over to them and said, "Now, remember what we agreed." The women stopped immediately.

On the fifth morning I had just begun my address when one of the elders stopped me and asked me to give him a chance to confess his sins. He said that he couldn't endure the burden any longer. He confessed to lying, stealing and adultery. After the elder had resumed his seat and I had just got nicely started again, an evangelist cried out that he simply could not hold back and that I must give him a chance to confess his sins. He proceeded to tell how he had had a very serious quarrel with another evangelist. For a long time the two of them had not been on speaking terms with one another. The foreign missionary, unaware of the difference between them, had sent them to an out-station to conduct a communion service. He realized now how awful had been his sin in administering that sacred rite while nursing hatred of his Christian brother in his heart. What had made matters worse, all the Christians at that service had known that the two of them were enemies. He concluded by absolving the other of all blame and assuming the whole burden of guilt to himself,

I proceeded with my address and again had only been speaking for a few minutes when the other evangelist broke in and begged me to let him have a moment or two. It was he who was to blame for the quarrel, he said; his brother evangelist was entirely innocent. After that I saw that it was useless for me to go on speaking. The movement continued throughout the remaining meetings.

On the last day the large tent, which had been built especially for the meetings, was crammed to capacity. Among the many who testified that day to God's wonderful dealing with them during the meetings was the elder whose confession had started that remarkable movement on the fifth morning. "I believe," he cried, "that I'm the happiest man in the tent today. My elder brother, as many of you know, was a notoriously wicked man. He wouldn't allow me even to mention the name of Jesus in his presence. I didn't dare open my mouth lest he should kill me. Yet today he came to me and asked me if there were any possible hope that Jesus would have mercy upon so great a sinner as he. You can just imagine what an inexpressible joy it was for me to lay before my brother, right there and then, the way of salvation and see him accept Jesus as his Lord and Savior. Don't you think I have good reason for being the happiest man in the tent today?"

As I was nearing Hwanghsien, in the cart, I was met by Dr. A—— with his children and several of the evangelists. After the usual greetings had been exchanged, one of the evangelists asked me: "Do you expect that the Holy Spirit will use you here to bless us with revival power as He did in Manchuria?" "Why, of course," I replied, "the Holy Spirit is always only too willing to revive His people, irrespective of their location. It doesn't depend upon Him. It depends upon you. Are you ready or not?" Nothing more was said on the subject at the time, and we continued on our way to the city.

On the second morning the evangelist, who had put the above question to me, broke down in his prayer. He said that twenty-seven men and women had been turned over to him to be prepared for baptism; but that he was unworthy to teach them as he had not yet been filled with the Holy Spirit. He needed to be first taught himself, he declared, before he could presume to teach others.

At the breakfast table, on the sixth morning, Dr. A—— told me that that night two of the Chinese leaders, one of whom was the evangelist already referred to, had wakened him up long after midnight to get him to pray with them. "Mr. Goforth has been here five days already," they said, "and yet there has been no real sign of revival. We're so troubled by the thought that the Lord might pass us by that we can't sleep." When I heard that I was greatly encouraged. I felt sure that God's time for favor was close at hand.

Yet, during the forenoon meeting that day there was no marked movement. In the afternoon I spoke on the Spirit's help in prayer, taking as my text Rom. viii. 26, 27. During the opening session for prayer and confession that followed my address I became aware of an ever-increasing tension. For about the first twenty minutes the people seemed to vie with one another in their eagerness to pray. Sometimes there would be two, sometimes three or even four people praying at the same time. But, as the sense of tension increased, the praying gradually died away. Finally, it seemed as if no one dared to pray. The presence of God seemed completely to fill the building.

How long the silence continued I am unable to say, but at last the tension was broken by a voice crying, "O Lord, you've come!" It was the evangelist referred to above. Instantly the cry was taken up all over the audience. Some fell to their knees and began confessing their sins. Others started to sing praises. Every one seemed to be praying or singing or confessing, quite apart from any thought of those around them. Though it was the most complete disorder it seemed to be the most perfect order. After this had gone on for an hour I felt that I ought to close the meeting. In a loud voice I pronounced the benediction, and told the people that the meeting was over. Not a soul appeared to hear me. At any rate, no one paid any heed to me. So for an hour and a half longer the movement continued, sweeping everything before it. I have never known intercessory prayer rise to such a height of intensity as during the latter part of this service. Even small schoolboys, with the tears trickling down their cheeks, were seen praying for their unsaved parents and friends back home.

It was among the boys of the High School, however, that the movement seemed to sweep with the greatest power. Unknown to the missionaries, or even to the Chinese teachers, the boys had formed an infidel club. All the older boys, it appeared, were members of this club. In their secret meetings they would read together certain infidel books, reprinted in Japan, which they had managed to smuggle into the school. When the fire touched their hearts, these boys came one after another and flung themselves down before the platform, confessing their sin of unbelief and pleading with God to renew their faith. The leader of the club was so agonized that I thought he would break his hands over the back of the bench in front of him. "Lord Jesus!" I heard him cry, "get ready a whip, put lots of cords in it and drive this devil of unbelief out of my heart."

By three o'clock next morning all those people, men, women and children, were back in the church, where they prayed and sang praises till sunrise. It was the middle of winter, and there were no fires in the building, yet they did not seem to mind. When I came before them at ten o'clock to lead the regular meeting there was a new light in their faces. They had seen visions at that morning watch. When I left Hwanghsien I was assured that there was not a single man, woman or student left unconverted in the congregation.

Years later, I was asked, on a certain occasion, to address a large officers' training school in Peking. I took as my subject: "The Christianity of General Feng." After I had spoken, eighty-four of those young men declared that they were going to read the Bible in order to find out the secret of the revolution which had been wrought in the life of that remarkable man. As I was about to leave I happened to notice one of the young officers, with a New Testament open in his hand, talking earnestly with a group of his fellow-students. "Men," I overheard him say, "there's nothing can save our country but this Book of God!" Then, noticing me, he bowed and said, "Do you remember me?" "I'm afraid I don't," I replied. "But you surely remember Hwanghsien," he went on. "I was attending the mission school there when you conducted those revival meetings, years ago. It was on that memorable sixth evening that I had the devil of unbelief burnt out of my heart. Naturally I can never forget that time."

Every imaginable obstacle seemed to be present at Pingtuchow to hinder the work of the Holy Spirit. For one thing, conditions in the High School were about as bad as they could be. The head-master was an ex-Presbyterian elder. In 1900 this man had denied his Lord to save his life. The matter had been brought up before the Presbytery, even so kindly a man as Dr. Corbett having felt that some notice should be taken of so serious a case. In the midst of the discussion the elder had flown into a rage and denounced the whole Presbytery. After that there was nothing else for it but to put him under suspension. The man was a very able scholar, however, and he had immediately been taken up by the Baptist Mission and appointed principal of the large High School at Pingtuchow. It was a most unwise move. A man in that unrepentant state was the very last person for such a responsible position. He had only been in charge of the school for a few months when a spirit of mutiny began to appear among the boys. About the third day of the meetings it became quite evident that the Holy Spirit was working among the scholars. Yet, whenever a boy made a confession, the principal would immediately follow, saying, "O Lord, comfort his heart. He's a good boy. He has really nothing to worry about."

The native pastor of the Pingtuchow church was always on the platform with me during the services. I was conscious that somehow he was not a help to me. One day, at the close of the forenoon service, he announced: "I wish all Chinese leaders and the missionaries of our church to remain after the meeting is dismissed." It seems that after the rest of us had left, he said: "My reason for asking you people to stay behind is that we may have special prayer for Mr. Goforth. His views on baptism are all wrong and must surely hinder the Lord." At that, I am told, one of the missionaries immediately jumped to his feet and cried: "In God's name, brethren, let's get down on our knees. It's not Mr. Goforth's views on baptism that are the cause of hindrance amongst us. It is our own sin."

But it was not until the sixth morning that one of the visiting missionaries made me aware of what was, perhaps, the most serious obstacle of all. This missionary said to me: "We believe that you are working in the dark. The hindrance here is far more serious than you imagine. The missionary who is in charge of this station at present is at deadly enmity with the one who has just gone home on furlough. This one has written to the Board asking them not to allow the other back to the field; while the other has approached the Board in person to urge the recall of the one here. The quarrel is common property among the Chinese leaders, and they have all taken sides, some for one, some for the other. The Chinese pastor hates the missionary who is here now, and boldly proclaims his allegiance to the one who has gone home. We missionaries have consulted together, and I have been sent to ask your advice as to whether we should not do our utmost to bring the different parties together." I at once said, "No, don't interfere. Leave the matter in God's hands."

My subject at the missionary prayer-meeting that morning was, "Have faith in God" (Mark ii. 22). Before I had concluded my talk, the missionary, who was concerned in the quarrel, interrupted me saying, "By the grace of God everything that I can straighten out shall be straightened out this day before sunset." At the close of the prayer-meeting the first thing he did was to send for the Chinese pastor and make matters right with him. Following which he wrote a letter to the Board retracting everything that he had said about his brother missionary. At the service that evening the native pastor took the initiative and went and shook hands with the missionary before all the people.

At the forenoon service on the seventh day the principal of the Boys' School came up on the platform and asked me, in a peculiar manner, for permission to confess his sin. I told him that he had perfect liberty to confess any hindering sin which the Holy Spirit prompted him to get rid of. "My great sin," he began, "has been that I have hated the foreign nations without praying for them. Take the Japanese, for example. Think of the injury that they have done to China!" He then proceeded to enumerate all the real or fancied wrongs which he claimed Japan had heaped upon China. "Yes," he said, "my great sin has been that I have hated the Japanese without praying for them." He went on to tell how Germany had injured China in various ways. His sin, he said, had been that he hated the Germans without praying for them. Then there was America. By her stringent immigration laws she had cruelly humiliated the poor Chinese people. He had sinned in hating the Americans without praying for them. There were several Swedish missionaries in the audience. "I don't think," he said patronizingly, "that we have anything in particular against the Swedish nation. At any rate, they're too small to do us any harm, even if they wished to."

But all this was merely by way of introduction. Like a true orator, he was working towards a climax. Continuing, he said: "There was a certain Englishman in China named Marjory. He was employed by a mandarin down south to cast a cannon. The mandarin supplied him with the right kind of metal, but, being a pig-headed Englishman, he insisted upon using a metal of his own choosing. The cannon was finally cast, and the mandarin sent about twenty of his men to test it. On being fired off, the cannon burst and blew those twenty men to bits. The official was so enraged that he drew his sword and killed Marjory. Then the British came down upon China and forced that cursed opium upon us. When the war was over, the British exacted an enormous indemnity from China, and their plea was, 'You have killed Marjory and let his poor wife and mother starve.' But how could I help but think of those twenty Chinese wives and mothers who were left to starve because of an Englishman's pig-headedness? It enraged me against the British, and I didn't pray for them."

At this juncture I laid a hand on the man's shoulder, and said: "Brother, you know perfectly well that there is not one atom of truth in what you say about Marjory. Furthermore, you are not confessing sin. You are not being prompted by the Holy Spirit. You are merely taking advantage of this opportunity to vent your spite upon other people." At that the High School boys rose in a fury. I had insulted them by questioning the veracity of their principal. Shouting and yelling and kicking they left the church. I thought they would kick the church door off its hinges as they went out. Yet, strangely enough, a mighty conviction seemed to fall upon all who remained.

After the meeting I was discussing the incident with one of the lady missionaries. Her face was wet with tears. "Why are you taking on like that?" I asked. "Have you forgotten the subject of our prayer-meeting the other morning, 'Have faith in God'? Do you imagine that God is going to allow His Son to be disgraced in this fashion? It cannot be. I believe that, before these meetings end,

He will bring those boys back in a body to confess their sin and honor Him." "Oh, I wish I had your faith," she replied, still very doubtful.

After leaving the church that day the boys went through a time of terrible searching by the Holy Spirit. That night many of them could not sleep. On the eighth morning they stood up before the church in a body and acknowledged their fault. And, to crown the devil's defeat, the principal himself came up to the front, weeping, and confessed his sin.

At the final meeting, just as I was about to pronounce the benediction, the Chinese pastor intimated that he wished to say a few words. "Mr. Goforth," he said, "your addresses these days have shown us that you have a wonderful knowledge of the Bible. But allow me, as an insignificant Chinese brother, to beg of you that in the future, as you search the Scriptures, you will be careful to note what the Lord says regarding true views on baptism." It was an awkward situation. There were a number of Presbyterian leaders and representatives of other denominations in the audience. It looked like the devil's move to bring on a controversy and spoil everything. I decided to risk silence, and pronounced the benediction. Then I turned to the pastor and said quietly: "During the years that I have been leading these meetings I have been among Episcopalians, Congregationalists, Methodists, Presbyterians, Baptists and members of many other denominations, and I have found that no amount of baptismal water can keep the devil out of the hearts and lives of Christians."

Three years after these meetings were held it was reported that about three thousand had been added to the church in that region.

Chapter XII

HOW REVIVAL CAME TO THE SCHOOLS IN KIANGSU

I was invited to Nanking in the early spring of 1909 to lead a nine days' series of meetings. The Christians there were faced with the problem of finding a building large enough to hold the crowds which were expected to attend. The Friends owned the largest church in the city, and it would only seat six hundred. The Chinese leaders proposed to erect a large mat pavilion, but the missionaries pointed out that at that time of the year it would probably rain every day, in which case a pavilion would be out of the question. To this the Chinese replied that they would have to trust the Lord for the weather. The missionaries gave way and a pavilion with a seating capacity of 1,400 was erected.

I arrived at Nanking the day before the meetings were to begin. Rain was pouring down, and it looked as if it might continue to do so indefinitely. The first thing I did was to go and inspect the tent. It was leaking like a sieve. There was not a dry place where one could sit down. Next day the meetings opened and throughout the whole nine days not a drop of rain entered the pavilion. Some days, indeed, the weather looked very threatening. It seemed as if at any moment the pent-up torrents might be let loose. Still, the rain held off. The meetings came to an end and for two days it poured continuously.

On the evening of the third day the schoolgirls of the Adventist[1] Mission came under deep conviction while at worship in the school. In the tent, on the following morning, the prayers of these girls sounded a new and startling note. On the fourth evening the girls in the Friends' School were greatly moved. The next day the girls of the Presbyterian School all gave way.

[1] Not to be confused with the Seventh Day Adventists.

At the prayer-meeting in the Union High School, on the seventh morning, Mr. Meiggs, the principal, asked the boys how it was that they had as yet shown no signs of conviction. One of the leading students stood up. "Since you've asked us, principal," he said, "we will be plain with you. We know perfectly well that these meetings were arranged especially for our benefit. You foreign missionaries act as if you had no sin; and as if we Chinese were the only sinners to be found." Mr. Meiggs burst into tears. "Young men," he cried, "if you have seen anything wrong in me, tell me and I'll acknowledge it. If I have injured any of you, tell me and I will go and kow-tow to you." At his words the boys melted, and there followed an hour of the most sweeping conviction.

The last to be brought into the movement were the girls of the Episcopal Methodist School. The school buildings were just over the compound wall from where I stayed. It was at their prayer-meeting on the eighth evening that the girls broke down. Their piercing cries of conviction kept me awake till long after midnight.

On the day of my arrival at Nanking I had remarked on the unusual length of the great Oregon pine planks with which the platform in the tent was being constructed. I had expressed the fear then that they were going to take up far too much room in the pavilion and had suggested that they should be sawn in two. The reply had been that that was impossible as the planks were borrowed. When we came to the last day of the meetings I had abundant reason to be thankful that the platform was as roomy as it was. There were fully 1,500 people in the tent that day. Hundreds had to be turned away. The forenoon meeting lasted for four hours. I gave a brief address, and the remainder of the time was taken up with prayer and confession.

The unusual feature about the meetings this day was that every one seemed to want to come up on the platform to confess. I had never made any suggestion in that direction. In fact, I prefer that confessions should be given from the audience, while in prayer, and that they should be as unobtrusive as possible. Yet this day the whole trend was towards the platform. The crush was so great that it was found necessary to erect another stairway up to the platform. I obtained the services of another missionary, and he stood at one end of the platform and I at the other. The people gave their confessions facing the audience; then they usually turned to one or the other of us and asked us to pray for them.

At ten minutes to three that afternoon I went up on the platform to open the second meeting. Already hundreds of people were crowding towards the front, seeking for an opportunity to confess. I saw immediately that it was useless for me to think of giving an address. I got five other missionaries to help me, and we stationed ourselves on different parts of the platform. Sometimes there would be as many as thirty people up on the platform at a time, with, perhaps, half a dozen missionaries among them. Occasionally we would see a group of schoolgirls, with their heads all huddled together, ashamed at being seen by the great audience. But when their turn came their voices would ring out over the crowd. "You people needn't imagine," they would say, "that we want to come up on this platform and be stared at. For days we have tried to find peace by confessing our sins in private. But it is no use. We know this is the only way."

At ten minutes to nine, exactly six hours after the meeting had opened, I was compelled to leave in order to catch the steamer for Peking, where another series of meetings was awaiting me. As I left the tent scores of people were still waiting for a chance to confess.

Some of those confessions stand out in my memory as clearly now as when I listened to them twenty years ago. One schoolgirl said: "My father has a terrible temper. At school I was led to believe in Jesus, but I was in such fear of my father that I did not dare tell him about it. When my parents went to the temple to worship the gods they took me with them, and I said nothing. When they went to the theatre they always asked me to accompany them, and I was afraid to refuse. When they gambled at cards, I was a coward and joined in. But I'm going home today to confess Jesus to my people. Won't you all pray for me?"

The Chinese pastor of one of the Nanking churches broke down completely at one of the meetings. "For the first two days of these meetings," he said, "I did not realize that I had any sin. I got nothing out of Mr. Goforth's addresses. Then, on the third day, he spoke on the Laodicean condition. That searched me through and through. For the first time I saw myself as I was. Six months ago I had a quarrel with my son. In my temper I said things that I ought not to have said. Afterwards I was too ashamed to hold family worship. For six months now we have had no family worship in our home. If any of my family had died during that time, in their sin, I believe that God would have held me accountable."

One man, as he was about to confess, was quite overcome. The whole platform shook with his sobs. I thought that it must be a case of murder that was coming out. Finally, regaining his composure, he said: "When I first believed in Jesus the devil said to me, 'There's no need for you to testify or to preach the Gospel to others. That's the work of pastors and evangelists.' For seven years I've followed the devil's advice. I shudder to think of how many souls I have murdered."

There was a certain evangelist who had been used in a remarkable manner in the saving of souls and in quickening the churches. But for a year back, though he seemed as earnest as ever, there had been a marked lack of results in his work. The missionaries could not account for it. On the last day of the meetings the evangelist came up on the platform, greatly broken up, and confessed to having broken the seventh commandment.

Another evangelist confessed that the gown he was wearing had been acquired by unlawful means. He tore

the garment off, threw it down on the platform and
walked away without it.

An ex-preacher, who had gone into business and
acquired considerable wealth, cried out: "There is no
telling how many souls I have murdered, because I gave
up the preaching of the Gospel and followed my covetous
heart."

There was one of the Chinese leaders who had done
not a little to hinder the progress of the meetings. At the
first few services he had heard many confessions from
his own people, but none from the foreign missionaries.
The devil worked him up, and he went around among the
people, saying, "We are just a lot of fools. The foreign
missionaries have sins just the same as we have; but they
won't demean themselves by confessing them. Their
reputations are too valuable." In this way, by appealing
to their pride, he had managed to gather around him a
considerable number of the leaders. At the last meeting
this man was searched as by fire. As he stood there on
the platform he seemed to be in a veritable agony. He
said that the sight of five or six missionaries up on the
platform at one time, waiting their turn to confess, had
cut him to the quick. He had realized, then, that the
devil had simply used him as his cat's-paw.

But perhaps the most remarkable confession of all was
that of an evangelist who had charge of an important
church in a neighbouring city. Asking his mother to
stand up, the evangelist went over all the bad temper and
unfilial conduct which he had displayed towards her, and
begged her forgiveness. He then told of how shamefully
he had treated his wife. "My wife," he said, "has not had
any educational advantages. She cannot even read. And
sometimes, when I compare her with these beautiful, intelligent High School girls, I think to myself, would that
she would die off, and give me a chance to marry one of
these brilliant girls instead. I am going home now to
confess my sin to my wife, and I vow to God that henceforth I will love her as I ought."

"The love of Christ," he went on, "has not constrained me in my ministry. When I give an address on Sunday, the people praise me and say that I have done well. Even the foreign missionaries sometimes compliment me on what they call my splendid preaching. But it is all on the surface. I have no love for souls in my heart. If they all perished, it would make no difference to me. . . . For a long time I have been using the church collections for myself. The first Sunday after I return home I shall confess to my congregation and make full restitution. . . I have a younger brother who is an opium sot and a beggar. It is all due to my harshness. I never tried to win him with love. I don't know where he is, but I shan't rest till I find him."

The evangelist kept to his word. After the meetings were over he went back to his own church and confessed everything to his people; and I understand that not long afterwards a revival began. He then started out to look for his brother. He went from city to city, and found his brother, finally, in the last stages of destitution, on the streets of Yangchow. He so pleaded with him that the other, far gone though he was, yielded to Christ. The two of them went back home together, and the last I heard was that the younger brother had found steady employment in the mission hospital.

I came to Hsuchowfu in the fall of 1915 to conduct a series of meetings running over fifteen days. The missionaries had been having considerable difficulty with their High School. There were over 150 students in the school, two-thirds of whom were from non-Christian families. The missionary head-master was finding it almost impossible to maintain any sort of discipline. In fact, not long before my arrival, matters had come to such a pass that he had decided to expel a dozen of the boys at the end of the year. He expressed the hope to me, though, that the Lord would so change the hearts of those boys that he would feel justified in reversing his decision.

To add to the trouble, it had been found necessary to dismiss one of the teachers. The teacher had been greatly chagrined over his loss of "face," and had told his friends that if the missionaries ever wanted to get him back to the church they would have to bring five hundred yoke of oxen to drag him there. I heard, too, that one of the High School students, on learning that I had been invited to come and conduct a series of revival meetings, said, "Well, if that man can melt bars of iron with his words, then perhaps he can hope to do something with us students."

On the third day of the meetings, one of the students came up on the platform, greatly broken up. He claimed that the non-Christian boys in the school were not being saved because of the poor example that he as a Christian, had been setting. He confessed to a number of things and, generally, gave one to understand that he was an exceedingly bad boy. After the meeting I made inquiries, and learned that he was the son of one of the deacons and the best boy in the school. That afternoon the boys were called together for an hour of study. The principal noticed that this boy's seat was empty. He went to his room and found him in tears, praying with the most intense earnestness for the salvation of his fellow-students. At the study hour, the following morning, the deacon's son again failed to put in an appearance. The principal again went to his room and found him praying in the same agonizing way.

From day to day there were indications of the Spirit's power; but it was not until a full week had passed that I began to notice anything out of the ordinary. At the missionary prayer-meeting on the eighth morning all present seemed to be deeply moved. No one could pray without breaking down. The one thought running through the prayers of the missionaries was that the church was in its present state because too little of the love of God had been manifested in their lives.

At the afternoon meeting, on the tenth day, there was a most unusual sense of the presence and power of God; but, as yet, no great brokenness. It was just that one felt, somehow, that the Spirit of God was in supreme control. It was well on to nine o'clock in the evening when the meeting finally broke up. That night many of the unconverted students wept all night over their sins, the Christian boys doing what they could to comfort them.

On the eleventh morning, I had just been speaking a few minutes when one of the boys cried out, "Please be patient a moment, and let me confess my sins." He made his confession, and I had just got nicely started again when another boy broke in and asked me to let him have a chance to confess his sins. I saw then that it was useless for me to go on with my address. I threw the meeting open, and many of the boys took advantage of the opportunity. Each one, on ending his confession, would ask me to pray for him. After I had responded to the first few I would say: "Now, will some one who has come through to victory pray for our young brother?" As a rule, it would be a fellow-student who would respond.

At the afternoon meeting, which was just a repetition of the one in the morning, a striking-looking gentleman, evidently under intense conviction, claimed that the church was in its miserable condition because of his wrong living. A missionary whispered excitedly to me that this was the ex-teacher. A day or so later, the teacher was put to a severe test. There was a certain back-slidden medical practitioner in the city who had been making a most decided nuisance of himself during the meetings by always trying to get his prayer in before anyone else, whenever an opportunity presented itself. It was a well-known fact that, in spite of his profession of Christianity, he was living a life of vice. He was a little late in arriving at one of the early morning prayer-meetings, but, nothing daunted, he was pressing up to the front as usual, when the ex-teacher put out a restraining hand, saying, "Brother, sit down here. Don't disturb the meeting." His only reply was a terrific blow on the chest. The next moment the medical practitioner was stalking out of the building, foaming mad.

The surprising thing about it all was that the teacher made no attempt to retaliate. He was a great muscular fellow, while the other was an insignificant specimen, about half his size. The teacher, moreover, had always been noted for his ferocious temper. Speaking of the incident later to several of us, he said: "I know that the Holy Spirit must have filled me that night that I confessed my sin. Had He not done so, do you suppose that I would have received the blow from that wretch without moving a muscle or saying a word. If it had happened a few days before I would have leaped upon him and choked him to death." At the closing meeting the teacher gave a striking testimony, in which he told of what great things God had done for himself and his family. Standing around him were his father and mother, his wife and children and brothers, fourteen in all. "Here we are," he cried, "all saved! All praising God!"

At the missionary prayer-meeting, on the twelfth morning, we heard from the principal of the Girls' School how that, as far as she knew, every girl in the school had been brought to Christ. She said that the last to yield was a big, ugly, undisciplined girl, who had broken every rule in the school. This girl, when she was finally convicted, found it almost impossible to contain herself. She first went and apologized to all the teachers, even getting down and kow-towing to them. Afterwards she went to all her schoolmates, whom she had offended, and asked their forgiveness. During this scene, said the principal, the Confucian teacher, a fine old scholar who had resisted all approaches of the Gospel by saying that "he was a pupil of the great sage Confucius, and had no need of this Western Jesus," was deeply touched. Amazed at the unbelievable change that had come over that ugly-dispositioned girl, the tears began to roll down his cheeks, and he cried, "Jesus has conquered. He is God. I yield."

As the principal ended her story, someone said, "Oh! if only the same thing would happen over at the Boys' School!" The words had hardly been spoken when Mrs. G——, the wife of the principal of the Boys' School, burst into the room, evidently in great excitement. Addressing me, she said: "Do please go over to the High School and see what you can do there. For an hour the boys have been down on their faces, weeping. My husband and the other teachers are just as bad as any of them." Hurrying over to the school, I found it as Mrs. G—— had said. I asked the principal how the movement had started and he said: "This morning I told all the Christian boys to go over to the prayer-meeting in the church, and asked the boys who were unconverted to remain with me here. Some seventy odd remained. I talked to them for a little while, and then I said, 'Now, boys, just tell God all about it.' Presently the worst boy in the school, the leader in every prank and devilry, came under conviction and confessed his sins. This started the others, and it wasn't long before the whole seventy of them had given way completely."

For about half an hour I made no attempt to interfere, and then, judging that the boys were through confessing, I started up some choruses. In a little while we had the whole crowd back in their seats. Then I spoke to them for a few minutes from 2 Cor. v. 14. I told them about the love of Christ in His being made sin for them, and paying the penalty due for their transgressions. Then I went on to tell of how He had risen from the dead, and that through faith in His finished work we might rise with Him. "Now, young men," I said, "if you will take your stand by Christ today, just stand up." With that every boy, but one, jumped to his feet.

Afterwards pipes were smashed, cigarettes and tobacco thrown away, and stolen knives and pencils and handkerchiefs restored to their owners. The boy who had not stood up at my invitation was exceedingly troubled all that day and on through the following night. If anyone would mention Jesus to him, he would fly into a rage. But about four o'clock in the morning he came into victory. He went immediately to his teacher to get permission to go back home and bring his people into the meetings. His father, he said, had died three months before in unbelief; and he had murdered his father's soul because he had been in a Christian school and had had a chance to tell his father of the way of salvation, but had not done so. His home was a good sixteen miles away, yet he was back again at the one o'clock meeting with a number of his friends and members of his family, eleven in all.

At the close of the meetings, eight of the High School boys asked for a special interview with me. I found that their one desire was to learn the secret of that power which would enable them to remain true to the stand which they had taken. The prayers of these boys and girls, so recently brought out from unbelief, were really remarkable for their keenness of perception. They prayed with apparently as clear a realization of the meaning of the Christian discipleship as those who had grown old in the faith. When I left, the teachers assured me that there was not a boy or girl in the schools who had not given convincing evidence of a saving faith in Jesus Christ.

Chapter XIII

INDISPENSABLE FACTORS IN REVIVAL

A MISSIONARY once remarked apologetically to me: "I have always longed for revival; but my station is so out-of-the-way that it is impossible for me to obtain the services of an evangelist." As if the Spirit of God is necessarily limited in His workings to a select few! We wish to state most emphatically as our conviction that God's revival may be had when we will and where we will. That peer of evangelists, Mr. C. G. Finney, believed that any body of Christian people, provided they whole-heartedly and unreservedly carried out God's will, could have revival. Mr. D. L. Moody was continually urging that Pentecost was merely a specimen day. Most certainly it is not to be misunderstood from these pages that the Orient is peculiarly suited to revival. We have seen audiences in the homelands moved in exactly the same way as in China. True, it usually takes longer. But, whether it takes a day or whether it takes a fortnight, the principle is clear that any group of seeking Christians may receive the full blessing of Pentecost.

Our reading of the Word of God makes it inconceivable to us that the Holy Spirit should be willing, even for a day, to delay His work. We may be sure that, where there is a lack of the fulness of God, it is ever due to man's lack of faith and obedience. If God the Holy Spirit is not glorifying Jesus Christ in the world today, as at Pentecost, it is we who are to blame. After all, what is revival but simply the Spirit of God fully controlling in the sur-rendered life? It must always be possible, then, when man yields. The sin of unyieldedness, alone, can keep us from revival.

But are we ready to receive Him? Do we value the Giver and the gift sufficiently? Are we ready to pay the

price of Holy Ghost revival? Take prayer for example.
The history of revival shows plainly that all movements
of the Spirit have started in prayer. Yet is it not right
there that many of us wilt and falter at the cost? The
Bible does not tell us very much of what went on in that
Upper Room in Jerusalem between our Lord's ascension
and the Day of Pentecost. But we may be reasonably
certain that that little band of disciples begrudged every
minute that was spent off their knees. There was so
much to be got rid of, so many hindering things to be
laid away, so much gold to be refined, so much dross to
be consumed. The Day of Pentecost told best what had
passed in that Upper Room. We know, too, that all sub-
sequent outpourings of the Spirit were linked with prayer.
"And when they prayed," Luke tells us, "the place was
shaken where they were assembled together, and they
were all filled with the Holy Spirit and spake the Word
of God with boldness" (Acts iv. 31).

The mighty spiritual upheavals in Reformation times,
came largely as the result of prayer. It is said of Luther
that he could get anything from God he asked for. Mary
Queen of Scots had a greater dread of the prayers of
John Knox than of all the armies of England. That
glorious movement of the Spirit which fused the dis-
cordant elements among the Moravians at Herrnhut in
1727, and transformed them into what has been the
mightiest evangelizing force in the world for the past
two centuries, was born in prayer. "Was there ever in
the whole of Church history," writes Bishop Hasse, "such
an astonishing prayer-meeting as that which, beginning
(at Herrnhut) in 1727, went on one hundred years? It is
something absolutely unique. It was known as the
'Hourly Intercession,' and it meant that by relays of
brethren and sisters prayer without ceasing was made
to God for all the works and wants of His Church. Prayer
of that kind always leads to action. In this case it kindled
a burning desire to make Christ's salvation known to the
heathen. It led to the beginning of modern foreign mis-

sions. From that one small village community more
than one hundred missionaries went out in twenty-five
years. We will look in vain elsewhere for anything to
match it in anything like the same extent."[1] But is there
any reason, may we ask, why the Moravian movement
should not be matched today? It is not likely that the
Eternal Spirit has grown weary. Surely we may count
on it that the blessing is waiting for us, if we will only
get down on our knees and ask for it.

Perhaps the most striking phase of the Wesleyan movement was the emphasis which its leaders laid on prayer.
Their regular practice was to pray from four to five in
the morning and from five to six in the evening. Great
figures like William Bramwell, however, would spend
half the night in prayer besides, and afterwards go
through a district like a flame of fire. If only the millions
of Methodists today would but esteem prayer as did their
great forefathers, what might not happen!

Finney depended more upon the prayers of fathers
Nash and Clary to bring down Holy Ghost revival than
upon his own resistless logic. So accustomed are we today to the Laodicean condition of the Church that the all-
pervading influence of prayer in Finney's time amazes us.
Imagine forty ministers and missionaries being thrust
into the Lord's harvest field as the result of prayer during
one revival in a Rochester High School! By 1857, Finney
was seeing fifty thousand a week turning to God. In many
cities there was no building large enough to hold the
prayer-meetings. It was at that time that the Fulton
Street prayer-meeting started in a side room in a church,
and in a few weeks had taxed the capacity of the entire
building to the utmost, and had even overflowed to
neighbouring churches.

In 1858, Mr. Spurgeon called his great congregation together and said: "The Spirit of God is saving multitudes
now in the United States. Since God is no respecter of
persons we will pray until He sends similar showers of

[1] John Greenfield, "Power from on High," pp. 25, 26.

blessing upon our land." The mighty revival of 1859 was the answer. Mr. Moody, it is said, would not accept an invitation to conduct a mission unless he were given positive assurance that the way would be prepared by prayer. In the south of Wales, shortly before the great revival there in the early years of the present century, three hundred extra prayer-groups were formed. Wales, in fact, became almost like one great prayer-meeting. What was the result? Within two months seventy thousand turned to the Lord.

At Calcutta, in 1902, two lady missionaries of the Khassia Hills Mission listened to an address on prayer by the late Dr. Torrey. They were so moved by it that when they went back to their people their one theme was prayer. The result was that, by the Spring of 1905, the Khassians were praying everywhere. Revival, of course, was inevitable. Within a few months, over eight thousand additions were made to the Church in that one section of India.

In an early chapter we pointed out how that it was intense, believing prayer that had so much to do with the revival which, in 1907, brought fifty thousand Koreans to Christ. We are convinced, too, that all movements of the Spirit in China which have come within our own experience, may be traced to prayer. After one particularly moving series of meetings a missionary remarked to me: "Since the Lord did so much with our small amount of praying, what might He not have done if we had prayed as we ought?" "What is the secret of revival?" a great evangelist was once asked. "There is no secret," he replied. "Revival always comes in answer to prayer."

We wish to affirm, too, that we can entertain no hope of a mighty, globe-encircling Holy Spirit revival without there being first a back-to-the-Bible movement. The Author of the Bible is being greatly dishonored these days by the doubt cast upon His Word. It must, indeed, be a cause of intense grief to Him that the Book which alone testifies of the Lord Jesus should be so lightly esteemed by man. Unless the Bible is to us in very truth the Word of God, our prayers can be naught but sheer mockery. There never has been a revival except where there have been Christian men and women thoroughly believing in and whole-heartedly pleading the promises of God.

The Sword of the Spirit, which is the Word of God, is the only weapon which has ever been mightily used in revival. Where it has been given for what it claims to be, the Word of God has always been like a sharp, two edged sword, like fire, and like a hammer that breaketh the rock in pieces. When Luther got the Scriptures translated into German, that country was lost to Rome. Moody did not possess the learning of the schools, but he did know his Bible; and it is certain that the world never has known, and doubtful if it ever will know, his equal as an apostle of souls.

During my student days in Toronto my one weapon, in the jails and slums, was the Bible. In China I have often given from thirty-five to forty addresses in a week, practically all of them being simply Bible rehearsals. In fact, I think I can safely say that, during the forty-one years that I have been on the foreign field, I have never once addressed a Chinese audience without an open Bible in my hand, from which I could say, "Thus saith the Lord!" I have always taken it for granted that the simple preaching of the Word would bring men to Christ. It has never failed me yet. My Chinese pastor, one of the most consecrated men I have ever met, was saved from a life of shame and vice by the first Gospel address which he ever heard me give.

My deepest regret, on reaching threescore years and ten, is that I have not devoted more time to the study of the Bible. Still, in less than nineteen years I have gone through the New Testament in Chinese fifty-five times. That prince of Bible-teachers, Dr. Campbell Morgan, has declared that he would not attempt to teach any book in the Bible unless he had first read it over at least fifty times. Some years ago, I understand, a gentleman attended the English Keswick and was so fired with a zeal for the Bible that in three years he read it through twelve times. One would imagine, of course, that he belonged to the leisured class. On the contrary, however, he began his day's work at the Motherwell steel plant at 5:30 a. m.

The Bible was not so neglected a Book when the great revivals of 1857-59 swept over the United States and Great Britain. Neither was it so neglected in Moody's time. During the late Manchu dynasty, scholars were expected to know the classics of their sages off by heart. How do the scholars of so-called Christian lands measure up to that standard as regards the "World's Great Classic"? It is nothing short of pathetic how so many, who come professedly to represent the Lord Jesus Christ in China, know so little of His Word. Thirty years ago the missionary ideal was to know the Bible so well that one would not have to carry around a concordance. Is the indifference to the Bible today on the part of so many missionaries due to the fact, perhaps, that they have discovered some better means with which to meet the needs of a sin-sick world?

Finally, the call to revival must be a call to exalt Jesus Christ in our hearts as King of kings and Lord of lords. He is like an Everest peak, rising from the level plain. There must be room only for Him, if we would have Him dwell with us at all. Every idol must be smashed; every darling Isaac laid on the altar; every urge of self denied. Then, and then only, can we expect the larger fields to open before us. It is said of Mahmoud, the great Moslem warrior that, in his trail of conquest through Northern India, it was his practice to destroy all idols which fell into his hands. He came at last to the city of Guggeratt, where there was an idol which was held in unusually high esteem by the people. The chief notables of the city came to the general and pleaded with him that he would spare to them this one idol. He might do as he wished with the others, they said, but if he took this god from them, too, they might just as well die. They pleaded with such intensity that, for a moment, the heart of the conqueror was touched. It seemed more than heartless to bereave these poor people of what was apparently life and death to them. Then he remembered his vow to spare not one idol. The will of Allah was plain. He had a sledge hammer brought to him, and with it he dealt the idol one terrific blow. To his amazement there poured from the rent in the image a stream of jewels and precious stones. The people had hidden their treasures in the image, hoping to move the conqueror to spare it. Consider what his loss would have been if he had stayed his hand at the sacrifice of that one last idol.

Was there ever such an incomparable opportunity for Christian leaders to get rid of their ecclesiastical idols and bring themselves into heart contact with the unsearchable riches of Christ as at the Missionary Conference in Edinburgh in 1910? There has been no Church gathering in modern times around which such expectations have centered. Missionary leaders had come from all parts of the world. It was the confident hope of many that a new era in missions had dawned. The subject for the last day was—"The Home Base." It provoked visions of endless possibilities. The home churches, empowered by a mighty Holy Ghost Revival, would send out men fitted as were Paul and Barnabas. With their enormous resources in men and means the world would be evangelized in a generation.

Alas! it was only a dream. Never have I experienced such keen pain and disappointment as I did that day. Of the many who addressed that great missionary gathering, not more than three emphasized God the Holy Spirit as the one essential factor in world evangelization. Listening to the addresses that day, one could not but conclude that the giving of the Gospel to lost mankind was largely a matter of better organization, better equipment, more men and women. Symptoms, indeed, were not lacking that a few more sparks might have precipitated an explosion. But no, the dethronement of the idol of ecclesiastical self-sufficiency was apparently too great a price to pay.

But, brethren, the Spirit of God is with us still. Pentecost is yet within our grasp. If revival is being withheld from us it is because some idol remains still enthroned; because we still insist in placing our reliance in human schemes; because we still refuse to face the unchangeable truth that "it is not by might, but BY MY SPIRIT."